WILLIAM NICHOLSON

The Retreat from Moscow

William Nicholson is the author of the play *Shadowlands*, which was made into a film starring Anthony Hopkins and Debra Winger. He received an Academy Award nomination for his screenplay for *Shadowlands* and has written numerous other screenplays as well as a forthcoming novel, *The Society of Others*, and a trilogy of children's fantasy adventure novels. He lives in London.

The Retreat from Moscow

THE

RETREAT FROM

MOSCOW

▼ ▼ ▼

A Play About a Family

WILLIAM NICHOLSON

ANCHOR BOOKS

A DIVISION OF RANDOM HOUSE, INC.

NEW YORK

AN ANCHOR BOOKS ORIGINAL, FEBRUARY 2004

Copyright © 2004 by William Nicholson

All rights reserved under International and Pan-American
Copyright Conventions. Published in the United States
by Anchor Books, a division of Random House, Inc.,
New York, and simultaneously in Canada
by Random House of Canada Limited, Toronto.

Anchor Books and colophon are registered trademarks
of Random House, Inc.

CAUTION: This play is protected in whole, in part, or in any form,
under the Copyright Laws of the United States of America, the British
Empire, including the Dominion of Canada, and all other countries of the
Copyright Union, and is subject to royalty. All rights, including professional,
amateur, motion picture, recitation, radio, television, and public reading
are strictly reserved. All inquiries concerning performance rights should be
addressed to the author's agent: Joyce Ketay, 1501 Broadway, Suite 1908,
New York, New York, 10036.

Grateful acknowledgment is made for permission to reprint the following: "The
Impulse" from "The Hill Wife" from *The Poetry of Robert Frost,* edited by Edward
Connery Lathem, copyright 1916, © 1969 by Henry Holt and Co., copyright
renewed 1944 by Robert Frost. Rights in the United Kingdom administered by
Jonathan Cape, London. Reprinted by permission of Henry Holt and Company,
LLC, The Estate of Robert Frost, and The Random House Group Limited.
"Autumn" by Rainer Maria Rilke, translated here courtesy of Hope Rosenthal. "The
Confirmation" from *Collected Poems* by Edwin Muir. Used by permission of the pub-
lisher, Faber and Faber, Ltd.

Library of Congress Cataloging-in-Publication Data
Nicholson, William.
The retreat from Moscow : a play / William Nicholson.
p.   cm.
ISBN 1-4000-7763-X (pbk.)
1. Married people—Drama. 2. Divorce—Drama.   I. Title.
PR6064.I235R48 2003
822'.914—dc22
2003063572

Book design by Debbie Glasserman

www.anchorbooks.com

Printed in the United States of America
10 9 8 7 6 5 4 3 2 1

PREFACE

Many years ago, when I was nineteen years old and in my first term at college, I fell in love. It took me most of that first term to pluck up the courage to reveal my love, but when at last I did, I found to my astonishment that I was loved in return. I realised then that I had found the one person in all the world who could make my unfinished life complete. I marvelled at my good fortune. As a lover, I was faithful and devoted. I wanted her happiness more than my own, because so long as I made her happy she would go on loving me, and so long as she went on loving me, I had all I wanted in life.

She left me in the summer term. I know now that the demand I made of her—that she make my life complete—was illegitimate, and tiresome. The love that left me as a gift landed on her as a burden. She fled.

I was devastated. The pain was so intense I could barely move, and certainly had no desire to speak. I flinched from the sight of anything that brought her back to me: places I had been with her, clothes I had worn with her, music I had played with her. Since this added up to just about everything, I entered a kind of blank of my own making.

In those days, my home was still my parents' house, and there I hid myself away. My mother saw my unhappiness and wanted to help me, so she reached out to me in the only way she knew: through poetry. My mother has loved poetry all her life, and has a remarkable memory for poems. She gathered together all the poems she knew on the subject of lost love, and made me an anthology to show me that others before me had suffered as I suffered. She typed out the poems and clipped them into a ring binder and gave them to me. I was not grateful. I didn't even read them. In the isolation of my pain, I refused consolation.

Time passed. I moved on to other relationships, other mistakes. And my parents' marriage began to disintegrate. By the time I was in my mid-twenties, I was watching helplessly as my good and gentle father found out that he could no longer live with my strong and loving mother. Caught between them, only wanting the pain to stop, I witnessed the devastation of two lives rending after thirty years of union. Good people in the pursuit of good lives can inflict torment too. How could I blame either of them? I understood too much.

My father left home. My mother was broken in half. A common enough occurrence, not the stuff of tragedy. Meanwhile, I was becoming a writer.

Writing is an odd enterprise. Why take the fragments of lived experience and rearrange them in some new pattern? Why tell stories at all? For a while I supposed the urge came from a need to tidy up the mess of life, to impose meaning on the meaningless. More recently I have come to see that I am in the grip of a greater drive, which I name with some hesitation, because it seems too grand. I am trying, clumsily, to reach the truth of my life. This is hard. Like everyone else, I tell lies all the time, most of all to myself. I lie about who I am and what I want and how much I hurt. I lie to survive. I tell a story of myself that I hope will make others love and admire me. But more and more, I write to strip away these lies, and say, Look, this is how it really is. What then? I look. I recognise the truth. That's all. No moral. No lesson. No consolation. And yet it's profoundly satisfying. This is the experience the great writers give me. It's what I'm trying to do in my own work.

One day I came upon the anthology my mother had made for me all those years ago, and read it, and was overwhelmed. Of course now I found in it the dreams and echoes of her own life, not my own callow affair. So I decided to write about the failure of my parents' marriage. This play is the result. It's not a documentary. I don't really know what happened inside their hearts and minds. But I know what's been going on inside my own heart and mind, so I know about the characters of my play, Alice and Edward and Jamie, because they're all me. I'm trying to tell the truth about the pain of loving badly, because I too have loved badly.

Both my parents are still alive, now well into their eighties. My father has found the life he wanted. My mother remains gallant and wise, and alone. She finds life difficult, but she endures. Both my parents have read my play, and wish it every success, but feel remote from it. As for me: I was forty before I married, and more honest than I used to be. My marriage has made me deeply happy. We have three children, now growing up. We do our best to keep telling each other the truth about what we want. My wife says she has my parents to thank for our happiness. So maybe some lessons can be learned.

William Nicholson
October 24, 2003

The Retreat from Moscow

The Retreat from Moscow was first produced at the Chichester Festival Theatre in October 1999.

It was first produced for the New York stage on October 23, 2003, at the Booth Theatre by Susan Quint Gallin, Stuart Thompson, Ron Kastner, True Love Productions, Mary Lu Roffe, and Jam Theatricals.

The cast was as follows:

EDWARD	John Lithgow
JAMIE	Ben Chaplin
ALICE	Eileen Atkins

Directed by Daniel Sullivan
Set design by John Lee Beatty
Costume design by Jane Greenwood
Lighting design by Brian MacDevitt
Original music and sound design by John Gromada
Production stage managed by Roy Harris

ACT ONE

▼ ▼ ▼

The stage in darkness.

Two armchairs. A table with three upright chairs. A sink, cooker, fridge, and cupboard.

Three people sit motionless in the darkness. EDWARD, *a schoolteacher in his late fifties, in one armchair. His wife,* ALICE, *about the same age, in the other. Their son,* JAMIE, *in his early thirties, at the table.*

All three actors remain onstage throughout. When one character is no longer present in a scene, he becomes still, and the lights go down on him. The audience can still see him, but the other characters cannot. The shadowed actor sits or stands, suspended in time, and does not react to what takes place around him, until the lights return him to the action.

Lights come up on EDWARD. *He reads from a book.*

EDWARD: "As men dropped in the intense cold, their bodies were stripped of clothing by their own comrades, and left naked in the snow, still alive."

(*Lights come up on* JAMIE, *sipping at a mug of coffee, listening.*)

"Others, having lost or burned their shoes, were marching with bare feet and legs. The frozen skin and muscles were exfoliating themselves, like successive layers of wax statues. The bones were exposed, but being frozen, were completely insensitive to pain. Some officers, suffering from diarrhoea, found themselves unable to do their trousers up. I myself helped one of these unfortunates to put his asterisk-asterisk-asterisk back, and button himself up. He was crying like a child."

JAMIE: I wonder what word he used.

EDWARD: Who knows? Something French.

JAMIE: Yes. I suppose it would be.

EDWARD: A surprisingly large number of the officers kept diaries. Over a hundred and fifty have survived. Remarkable, really, given the conditions on the retreat.

JAMIE: How many died?

EDWARD: Napoleon marched four hundred fifty thousand men across the Niemen. Less than twenty thousand came back. How was the drive down?

JAMIE: Not bad. I left just after five.

(*Both check their watches, making the same movement.*)

EDWARD: An hour and three-quarters. I wouldn't have thought there was that much traffic on a Saturday evening.

JAMIE: It took twenty minutes just getting through Tunbridge Wells.

EDWARD: Tunbridge Wells is slow.

JAMIE: I think I might have a bath.

EDWARD: Yes. Do.

JAMIE: Wash off the London grime.

(*He rises, and takes his coffee mug to the sink.*)

So everything's alright, then?

EDWARD: Much as ever. And you?

JAMIE: Busy.

EDWARD: Let's see if we can find a moment. Before you go back.

JAMIE: Sure.

(EDWARD *returns to his book. Lights go down on him.*)

(*Lights come up on* ALICE. JAMIE *walks across to stand behind her chair.*)

ALICE: It seems to me as I grow older that people become ruder. They say nobody's taught manners any more, but I don't think it's that. I think middle-aged women have become invisible. You have to be young, or rich, or beautiful, to be noticed at all. I don't quite know how to cope with it, except by getting angry, which I do more or less all the time these days. I've been having trouble with my printer. Did I tell you?

JAMIE: No. What's the problem?

ALICE: I dropped it.

JAMIE: Ah. They don't like that.

ALICE: *Sudden and swift and light as that*
The ties gave,

And he learned of finalities
   Besides the grave.

JAMIE: Auden?

ALICE: Robert Frost. A strange little poem called "The Impulse."
I'm putting it in my anthology under Lost Love.

JAMIE: How's the anthology coming along?

ALICE: Well, it isn't, really, until I can get the printer fixed. Did
you come down alone?

JAMIE: Yes. Have you got someone to look at it?

ALICE: Darling, there isn't anyone. People don't fix things any
more, they throw them away.

I rang every shop in the Yellow Pages, but all they wanted to do
was sell me a new one. I found a man at last who said, rather
grudgingly, "Bring it in," so I drove all the way to this hellish
industrial estate, where there was this hellish computer ware-
house, and I lugged the damned machine in through one of
those ferocious doors that try to crush you, and there was one
little man, all alone in this vast space, sitting at a keyboard,
going tick-tick-tick. No attempt to help me as I struggled in.
Not a word. Not a look. After a while I said, "I'm a customer.
Aren't you supposed to serve me?" He looked up and said,
"Well?" Just, "Well?" I said, "My printer's not working." I
showed him the page I'd brought in to explain the problem. I'd
been trying to print out a Browning poem, the one that ends—

Just when I seemed about to learn!
   Where is the thread now? Off again!
The old trick! Only I discern—

Infinite passion, and the pain
Of finite hearts that yearn.

That's going into Lost Love, too. It's turning out to be by far
the largest section in the anthology. Anyway, the printer had
left off the first two words or so of every line, which made the
poem rather modern, but not as good. The man in the ware-
house said, "That's not a printer problem. The printer's fine.
It's what you're doing that's wrong. You're the problem." He
actually said it, in those very words. "You're the problem."
"How do you know?" I said. "You haven't looked at the printer.
You haven't even switched it on." "I know," he said, "because
if a printer prints wrong, it's not the printer's fault." "Are you
the printer's mother?" I asked him. "Are you telling me that
printers never go wrong?" "I'm telling you," he said, "that if
the printer's printing, then the printer's fine." "But it's not
fine," I said. "It's not printing right. Well, actually, it is printing right, but it's not printing left." He didn't have an answer
to that. He went back to going tick-tick-tick. "Excuse me," I
said. "I'm not finished. I want you to look at my printer." He
paid me no attention whatsoever. So I picked up my printer,
to take it over to where he sat, and I dropped it.

It made a kind of tinkling noise. He looked up when he heard
that, and smiled a cruel little smile, and said, "Would you like
me to sell you a new printer?" I was so angry I wanted to hit
him. So I said to him, "You're the kind of man who doesn't
love anybody and nobody loves you. You've got no friends,
and your wife hates you, and your children never talk to you."
He looked quite surprised for a moment or two. Then he said,
"Do you know me from somewhere?"

JAMIE: Oh, Ma.

ALICE: What do you think I should do?

JAMIE: Buy another printer.

ALICE: I feel such a fool.

JAMIE: Is it alright if I have a bath?

ALICE: Yes, of course, darling. When are you going back?

JAMIE: After lunch tomorrow.

ALICE: Thank you for coming. I know how busy you are.

JAMIE: Don't be silly.

(*Lights fade on* JAMIE, *and come up on* EDWARD. *He looks up from his book.*)

EDWARD: They found Moscow empty, so they plundered it, which meant they were followed on the retreat by an enormous baggage train. This in turn was followed by raiding parties of Cossacks. When men were wounded, or frostbitten, and could no longer walk, orders were given to carry them on the baggage wagons. This slowed the wagons down, of course, and reduced the chances that the baggage train would make it to Smolensk.

So the wagon-drivers looked out for especially rutted ground, and then drove fast over it, so that the wounded would be jolted off the wagons, without anyone noticing. Once left behind on the road, they froze to death. This was understood to be an accident. It was an unspoken conspiracy, by the strong, against the weak. Nobody looked back.

ALICE: It's horrible, Edward. Why do you go on reading it?

EDWARD: It is horrible. But it's curiously compelling, too. I suppose because it exposes the way human beings behave in extremis. When it's a matter of survival, people show no mercy.

ALICE: What utter rot. History is full of people laying down their lives for others. What about Jesus Christ?

EDWARD: Oh, well. Jesus Christ.

ALICE: Don't just sit there and say, "Oh well, Jesus Christ."

EDWARD: Yes, but he was God. I mean, he knew he'd rise again.

ALICE: What difference does that make?

EDWARD: Well, he would have known it wasn't the end.

ALICE: So you think that made it easy for him?

EDWARD: No, not quite that—

ALICE: You try being crucified. See how you like it.

EDWARD: Well, of course, I wouldn't.

ALICE: Then stop talking such rot. Honestly, Edward, I hope you don't talk rot like that in your Religious Studies classes. Has Jamie said anything to you?

EDWARD: About what?

ALICE: About anything.

EDWARD: He told me how long it had taken him to drive down.

ALICE: He can't have.

EDWARD: Why not?

ALICE: Because it's such a stupid and pointless thing to talk about. Why would he say anything so ridiculously dull?

EDWARD: I asked him.

ALICE: You asked him?

EDWARD: Yes.

ALICE: You asked him how long it had taken him to drive down here?

EDWARD: Something like that.

ALICE: Why? Do you care?

EDWARD: People have conversations like that. It has its uses.

ALICE: Why? What uses?

EDWARD: Oh, I don't know. Settling down. That sort of thing.

ALICE: Edward, Jamie is your son. Your only child. You see him maybe once every three months. And all you can think of to say to him is, "How long did you take to drive down?"

EDWARD: He's only just got here. As you say, we haven't seen him for some time. You have to start somewhere.

ALICE: Why not ask him if he's got a girlfriend? When's he going to get married? What's happening about grandchildren?

EDWARD: I can't ask him that.

ALICE: All you have to do is give him an opening, and if he's got something to say, he'll say it. He's thirty-two, you know.

EDWARD: Yes. I know.

(*He puts a bookmark in his book, puts it down, and rises.*)

Cup of tea?

ALICE: He's mentioned a girl called Carrie a couple of times. I wonder what happened to her?

EDWARD: He's never mentioned her to me.

ALICE: I can't help worrying about him. Do you think he's happy? He used to laugh so much when he was little, and now he doesn't laugh, really. I think living alone is bad for people.

EDWARD: I'm not sure that I agree. I think he's happy in that flat of his.

ALICE: Do you? All on his own?

EDWARD: Well, there's that, of course. But he has it the way he wants it. No washing up to speak of. You use a plate, wash it, and there it is, ready to use again. You don't run out of milk, because you're the only one drinking it, so you know just how much there is left in the fridge. You can leave your book open on the table, and never lose your place. Just little things, I know, but they have their value.

ALICE: You sound as if you envy him.

EDWARD: Perhaps a part of me does.

ALICE: Well, it's a part of you you have to fight. It's not good for anyone, hiding in a hole and having everything be always the same. That's why you need me. Think what you would have missed if it wasn't for me. You'd never have gone to India, for a start.

EDWARD: That's true.

ALICE: You know what we should do? We should go back to India for our golden wedding. I know it's not for ages. We could save up.

EDWARD: We'd be far too old. I'd be seventy-five.

ALICE: That's nothing. They have astronauts older than that.

EDWARD: I'll make us some tea, then.

(*He goes to make tea.* ALICE *rises, and takes up Edward's book. She leafs through it without reading it.*)

ALICE: Have you done anything about Thursday?

EDWARD: What about Thursday?

ALICE: You've forgotten, haven't you?

EDWARD: Forgotten what?

ALICE: It's our anniversary.

EDWARD: Oh. Right. No, I hadn't forgotten.

ALICE: You haven't said anything.

EDWARD: Well, it isn't Thursday yet. It's only Saturday. Don't lose my place.

ALICE: So you have something in mind?

EDWARD: What do you mean?

ALICE: Will we go out for dinner?

EDWARD: If that's what you want.

ALICE: It isn't.

EDWARD: It isn't?

ALICE: No.

EDWARD: Alright, then. We won't go out.

(ALICE *opens the book at the bookmark, tilts the book so the book-mark slides to the floor, and closes it again.*)

ALICE: Oh, look. I've lost your place.

EDWARD: Never mind.

ALICE: No. Mind.

EDWARD: It's not important.

ALICE: What is?

EDWARD: Is something the matter?

ALICE: What do you think?

EDWARD: Well, something seems to be bothering you.

ALICE: You just don't get it, do you?

EDWARD: No. I don't think I do.

ALICE: I say, "Will we go out for dinner on our anniversary?" You say, "If that's what you want." I say, "It isn't." You say, "Then we won't." But I do want to go out for dinner on our anniversary. Why else do you think I suggested it?

EDWARD: Then why say you don't?

ALICE: Because I don't want to do it because I want to do it. I want to do it because you want to do it.

EDWARD: Oh. Right.

ALICE: So do you want to do it?

EDWARD: Yes. Why not?

ALICE: Then I'd like that.

EDWARD: We'll do that, then.

(ALICE *closes her eyes and bows her head.*)

　　　How was your day?

ALICE: I wish you wouldn't talk to me like that.

EDWARD: Like what?

ALICE: Like that.

EDWARD: I was only asking.

ALICE: What were you only asking?

EDWARD: Your day. How's it gone?

ALICE: How am I supposed to answer?

EDWARD: I think that rather depends.

ALICE: Fine. I'm supposed to say, "Fine." It's not a real question. It's not about me. I want you to ask about me.

(*Lights come up on* JAMIE.)

JAMIE: I'm having a bit of trouble with the bath. The water came out brown at first. I've been trying to empty it, but the water won't go away.

ALICE: (*To* EDWARD) You said you'd deal with that drain.

EDWARD: I will. I'll do it in the morning.

ALICE: If you're not going to do something you tell me you're going to do, could you please tell me you're not going to do it, so I know I have to do it myself?

EDWARD: I'll do it first thing.

JAMIE: Actually, it's not a problem, because the brownness is kind of sinking to the bottom.

ALICE: I don't know why I even bother asking you.

EDWARD: I've said I'll do it.

ALICE: But you don't, do you? What you actually do is the crossword. "Just half an hour," you say. Do you realise that's three and a half hours a week? That's one whole waking day a month. Twelve days a year. On Thursday we'll have been married thirty-three years, and you'll have spent—what is it? Three hundred and something?

EDWARD: Three hundred and ninety-six.

ALICE: Three hundred and ninety-six days, more than a whole year of our marriage, doing the crossword.

EDWARD: I haven't done the crossword every day.

ALICE: No, but you've wanted to. Will you be coming to mass in the morning, Jamie?

JAMIE: I don't think so, no.

ALICE: We can go to the eleven o'clock. You can sleep in.

JAMIE: You know I haven't been to mass for years now.

ALICE: Yes, but it's just a phase, isn't it?

JAMIE: It's not just a phase.

ALICE: You always had such a strong faith. These things don't go away.

JAMIE: I was a child. People change. The things you need when you're a child change.

ALICE: What rot you talk, Jamie. Where do you get it from?

I'm not a child, and I still go to mass. And anyway, it's got nothing to do with what anyone needs. It's to do with what's true.

JAMIE: I don't want to have this argument.

ALICE: You can say you don't believe in God till you're blue in the face. He's still there.

JAMIE: Yes, alright. For you, but not for me, okay? Let's leave it at that.

ALICE: But why not? Just give me one reason. Are you angry at him?

JAMIE: If I thought God existed I'd be angry, alright. I mean, take a look at the world he's supposed to have made.

ALICE: It's a beautiful world.

JAMIE: Full of miserable, starving, tortured, crippled people.

ALICE: But that's exactly why it has to be true. If this world was all there is, how could we bear it? Edward, you explain.

EDWARD: I think the general idea is that the misery in the world comes from man's inhumanity to man.

JAMIE: I'd better not let my bath get cold.

ALICE: Go on, Edward. Explain why God lets the misery happen.

EDWARD: Well, the fundamental premise in the argument is that God created us as free beings. He gave us free will. So he can't really stop us doing terrible things to each other without taking away our free will and turning us into puppets.

ALICE: There, you see. It's not God's fault. So you don't have to be angry at him. And you can come to mass with us in the morning.

JAMIE: I'm not angry with God. That's your idea, not mine. Since you insist on having this pointless argument, I'll try to explain the way I see it. I think the world is a frightening place, where things happen that aren't fair, and there isn't really any meaning to any of it, and at the end we get wiped out. We can't bear that, so we invent God and heaven to reassure ourselves that it'll all work out in the end. I don't think that's a bad thing to do. I happen to think it's not true. But maybe I'm wrong.

ALICE: Oh, you are, darling. You're as wrong as wrong can be. What a terrible way to think. Why on earth do you do it? It must make you so unhappy.

JAMIE: No, not really. And anyway, look at it the other way round. Why do you think what you think? Just so you can be happy?

ALICE: Well, yes, of course. Nobody wants to be unhappy.

JAMIE: Even if you're just making it all up?

ALICE: But I'm not. I promise you, darling, I'm right about this. Do you remember how you always hated it when I made you put out your light at eight-thirty, and then you went to stay with David Mallinson—we were living in Maidstone—and neither of you went to sleep till midnight, and you came home half-dead with exhaustion and said I'd been right all along? Well, this is like that.

JAMIE: It isn't like that at all. And anyway, I was nine years old.

ALICE: You tell him, Edward.

EDWARD: Tell him what?

ALICE: That God exists.

EDWARD: You can't tell people a thing like that. It doesn't work.

ALICE: Then what's the point of theology? What do you tell your boys at school?

EDWARD: I'm a history teacher. I do one class a week in Religious Studies. I don't claim to be an expert.

ALICE: Well, I won't argue with you, Jamie, it'll only make me cross. But let me tell you, you're not the first to think such rot, and find out in the end you're wrong.

> *But as I raved and grew more fierce and wild*
> > *At every word,*
> *Methoughts I heard one calling, 'Child!'*
> > *And I replied, 'My Lord'.*

JAMIE: George Herbert?

ALICE: Well done.

JAMIE: Yes. Well, I'll go and have this bath.

(*Lights go down on* JAMIE.)

(EDWARD *brings over two mugs of tea, and gives one to* ALICE. *He settles down in his armchair.*)

ALICE: I hate it when Jamie talks like that.

EDWARD: He has to think for himself.

ALICE: Of course he has to think for himself. But why does he have to think such horrible things? It makes me feel we've done something wrong.

EDWARD: I don't think I'll make it to mass tomorrow morning.

ALICE: Why not?

EDWARD: I have too much to do. All the Fifth Form papers to

mark. I'd rather get it done while I'm fresh. I can go to the six o'clock.

ALICE: Oh, well. Suit yourself.

(EDWARD *reaches for the newspaper, and takes out a pencil to do the crossword.*)

Do you have to do that?

EDWARD: No. Not if there's something more important.

ALICE: What about those papers you have to mark?

EDWARD: As I said, I prefer to do them in the morning. I'm quite tired now.

ALICE: Well, we could just talk. People do, you know.

EDWARD: Alright.

(*He puts the newspaper away. They drink their mugs of tea in silence.*)

ALICE: Well?

EDWARD: What?

ALICE: I'm waiting.

EDWARD: For what?

ALICE: For you to start. Talking doesn't just happen. You have to say something.

EDWARD: What do you want me to say?

ALICE: Edward, sometimes you make me want to scream. I really don't think I can stand this much longer.

EDWARD: I'm sorry. You don't make it easy, you know.

ALICE: Why should I make it easy? You're not a baby.

EDWARD: I just know that whatever I start to talk about will turn out to be wrong.

ALICE: I don't see why. Anyway, don't be so gutless. Talk about something you want to talk about.

EDWARD: Well . . . I've become fascinated by the eye-witness accounts of the—

ALICE: Not the retreat from Moscow. I'm sorry, I can't stand it.

(*He looks up at her for a brief moment, and then away.*)

I can't stand any of it.

EDWARD: I don't know what you want me to say.

ALICE: Can you stand it? Is this what you want?

EDWARD: No . . .

ALICE: So why don't you do something about it?

EDWARD: I don't know what to do.

ALICE: If this isn't what you want, then what is?

EDWARD: I want you to be happier.

ALICE: What about you?

EDWARD: And me, yes.

ALICE: You want to be happier?

EDWARD: Yes.

ALICE: So what would make you happier?

EDWARD: If you were happier.

ALICE: No. Talk about you.

EDWARD: I don't want anything special.

ALICE: But you do want something? There's something that two people can have that we haven't got, that you wish we had.

EDWARD: Yes . . .

ALICE: What is it? Describe to me how you'd like us to be.

EDWARD: I don't know how to explain.

ALICE: Think of a word. Any word. The first word that comes into your head.

EDWARD: Sunny.

ALICE: Sunny?

EDWARD: That's what came into my head.

ALICE: Sunny? The most you can ask for after thirty-three years of marriage is sunny?

EDWARD: It's only one word. There's others.

ALICE: Give me other words.

EDWARD: I don't want to do this.

ALICE: Please.

EDWARD: I'll only make things worse.

ALICE: I'm trying to understand what's happening to us, Edward. How will that make things worse?

EDWARD: Because whatever I say will be wrong.

ALICE: It can't be wrong if it's true.

EDWARD: Or not enough.

ALICE: What do you mean, not enough?

EDWARD: I don't know. Maybe it's all your poetry. Maybe I feel I can't compete.

ALICE: You're not supposed to compete with poems. You're supposed to say what you feel.

EDWARD: I do. But it's not enough.

ALICE: You don't say what you really feel. What you feel passionately about.

EDWARD: I'm nearly sixty, Alice. What do you want me to tell you?

ALICE: What's your age got to do with it?

EDWARD: You get tired . . .

ALICE: So you stop feeling?

EDWARD: No, of course not.

ALICE: You don't have passions any more?

EDWARD: I didn't say that.

ALICE: Well, do you? I don't see any evidence of it. What's happening, Edward?

EDWARD: I think . . . maybe . . . you want something I haven't got.

ALICE: What?

EDWARD: I always feel that somehow I'm in the wrong.

ALICE: I don't care about who's right or wrong. I just want you to be there. Here.

EDWARD: I am here.

ALICE: No. You're not. It's like somehow you've sneaked away while I wasn't looking. I don't know how else to explain it. It's as if you've taken the easy way out.

EDWARD: You think the easy way is wrong?

ALICE: Yes. Always. I don't want a sunny marriage. I want a real marriage. That's not easy. It takes hard work.

(EDWARD *rises and heads towards the cupboard.*)

Where are you going?

EDWARD: To put out the breakfast things.

(*He takes bowls and spoons from the cupboard.*)

ALICE: You're walking away from me. That's what you're doing. You're sneaking away.

EDWARD: Alice, it's getting late. I'm tired.

ALICE: I'm tired, too. But we can't go on like this. This isn't the life I want. Is this the life you want?

EDWARD: Not exactly.

ALICE: Then do something about it.

(EDWARD *starts to lay out the breakfast things on the table.*)

Why lay for breakfast? Nothing will have changed in the morning. Edward, I can't bear it. I want you to stop. Put those things down. Come over here.

(*He does as she asks. She rises, and takes both his hands in hers.*)

Look at me.

(*He looks at her.*)

You see, I just can't bear what's happening to us any longer.

(*He looks back at her, very uncomfortable.*)

Say something.

EDWARD: I don't understand where all this has come from.

ALICE: It's come from me. I want a real marriage.

EDWARD: I don't know what you mean by that. I'm sorry, but half the time I don't know what you're talking about.

ALICE: Yes, you do. That's just sneaking-away talk.

EDWARD: That's not true.

ALICE: Alright. I'll say something even you can understand. I love you.

EDWARD: Right.

ALICE: Do you love me?

EDWARD: You don't need to ask that.

ALICE: When did you last say it?

EDWARD: It's just assumed. It's just there.

ALICE: I want you to say it.

EDWARD: I can't now. It wouldn't mean anything.

ALICE: Why not?

EDWARD: I'd just be saying it because you asked me to say it.

ALICE: I don't mind.

EDWARD: This is childish, Alice.

ALICE: Just say it.

EDWARD: Why are you doing this? Why are you making everything into a problem? This isn't anything to do with me. This is all your problem.

(*WHACK!* ALICE *slaps him across the face.*)

ALICE: Don't ever say that again! You're part of this. You're involved, whether you like it or not.

(EDWARD *turns and walks away.*)

Do something. Say something. If you hate me, say you hate me. Say you want to leave me. Say you want to kill me. Tell me something real.

EDWARD: I'm tired. I want to go to bed. We'll talk about it in the morning.

(*Lights go down on* EDWARD.)

(ALICE *moves up close to the half-laid kitchen table, trembling all over. She grips the edge of the table. Suddenly she gives a sharp cry of frustration and anguish, and lifts up one side of the table, so that everything on it goes clattering to the floor.*)

(*Lights come up on* JAMIE.)

JAMIE: What happened?

ALICE: He's such a coward. Such a rotten sneaking coward.

JAMIE: You shouldn't go for him so much.

(*He starts to pick up the breakfast things.*)

ALICE: He should fight back. He's supposed to be the man. Why doesn't he fight back?

JAMIE: Is that what you want? A fight?

ALICE: I want a reaction. I want a real marriage. I've lived with him for more than half my life. He's so deep in me it's like he's part of me. We're all plaited and intertwined together. Nothing can undo that. So what is it he's so afraid of? Why does he walk away from me?

JAMIE: Because you go for him.

ALICE: I don't go for him. Well, I did hit him just now.

JAMIE: Oh, Ma.

ALICE: What else am I to do? How else can I get through to him? I feel that if I can only give him a big enough shock, he'll wake up.

JAMIE: Hitting him won't help.

ALICE: Well, what do you think I should do?

JAMIE: I think you should be nicer to him.

ALICE: Nicer? You sound like Edward.

JAMIE: I think you should stop going for him.

ALICE: You said that already.

JAMIE: But you don't listen, do you?

ALICE: Yes, well, we've all seen what a great success you've made of your love life.

(JAMIE *goes on clearing up in silence.*)

I'm sorry, darling. I didn't mean that.

JAMIE: Actually, you don't know anything about my love life.

ALICE: Don't I? Have you got a secret wife somewhere, and secret children?

JAMIE: You don't have to have a family to have a love life.

ALICE: Oh, that's just sex. You'll grow out of that.

JAMIE: Like I'll grow out of not believing in God.

ALICE: Yes.

JAMIE: Seems to be taking a long time.

ALICE: You must admit there's something odd about you living alone in that flat at your age.

JAMIE: I don't admit anything of the sort.

ALICE: You know Edward envies you.

JAMIE: Oh?

ALICE: He'd love to live in your flat and do the same things at the same time every day. That's what I rescued him from.

JAMIE: Well, don't try rescuing me.

ALICE: I do worry about you.

JAMIE: I worry about you.

ALICE: Why? Because Daddy and I have these little rows? These things happen in a marriage. We're working things out in our own way.

JAMIE: I'm just keeping well out of the line of fire.

ALICE: You know I love him, don't you? I love him even when I'm going for him, as you call it. After all these years it's got so that I can't imagine life without him. So you mustn't mind if we quarrel from time to time.

JAMIE: How did the breakfast things end up on the floor?

ALICE: I tipped the table up. I had to do something.

JAMIE: I thought maybe you'd thrown them at him.

ALICE: Oh, no. I wouldn't do that. Not cutlery.

JAMIE: I'm relieved to hear it.

(*He rises, replacing the last item on the table.*)

ALICE: I would have cleared it all up if you hadn't done it.

JAMIE: Well, it's done now.

ALICE: Thank you, darling.

JAMIE: So I'll see you in the morning, then.

ALICE: I think I may go to the early mass after all. Do you want me to wake you?

JAMIE: No. Let me sleep.

ALICE: Good night, then, darling.

(*She kisses him.*)

You have such a beautiful face. Can I tell you the poem I always think of when I look at you?

JAMIE: Go on, then.

ALICE: It's by Edwin Muir. I think he actually wrote it for his wife, but it always makes me think of you.

Yes, yours, my love, is the right human face.
I in my mind had waited for this long,
Seeing the false and searching for the true,
Then found you as a traveller finds a place
Of welcome suddenly amid the wrong
Valleys and rocks and twisting roads. But you,
What shall I call you? A fountain in a waste,
A well of water in a country dry,
Or anything that's honest and good, an eye
That makes the whole world bright . . .

JAMIE: It's not at all like me.

ALICE: Yes, it is. Mother knows best.

(*She kisses him again. Lights go down on* ALICE.)

(JAMIE *sits at the table.*)

(*Lights come up on* EDWARD, *who also takes a place at the table. Father and son proceed to have breakfast.*)

EDWARD: When do you have to go?

JAMIE: After lunch.

EDWARD: Right away after lunch?

JAMIE: Three-ish.

EDWARD: I don't suppose you could stay a little longer?

JAMIE: Well, no, I can't, really. Why?

EDWARD: It's just that things are rather coming to a head. I thought it might be better for Alice, if you were here.

JAMIE: I have to go out this evening.

EDWARD: Oh, well then.

JAMIE: Does it have to be today?

EDWARD: No, not really. It's just what we agreed.

JAMIE: What do you mean, things are coming to a head?

EDWARD: You know how it's been with Alice. For, oh, a long time now. Years. There was an incident a few weeks ago, at school. Maybe she told you about it.

JAMIE: No.

EDWARD: She found me in the staffroom. There was something I'd forgotten, or failed to do, something very minor. She went for me in front of my colleagues, which I consider unacceptable. What could I do? I walked out of the staffroom. To avoid the embarrassment of it. She came after me, saying, "Talk to me. Answer me. Look at me." I walked faster and faster, not really thinking where I was going. She followed. "Talk to me. Answer me. Look at me." I went out onto the playing fields. She followed. "Turn and face me, you coward. You can't run

32

for ever." And of course, the playing fields don't go on for ever. So I turned back, and there she was. I tried to walk past her, but she kept in my way, shouting at me. "Talk to me. Answer me. Look at me." Then she started to take off her clothes. She took off her jersey, and threw it at me. She was wearing a T-shirt underneath, like a teenager. She took that off, threw it at me. Then her skirt. Then her bra. It was unbearable. She looked pitiful, standing there, trembling, in the middle of the playing field. So of course I had to turn and face her. And she said, "There. I've made you look at me at last."

(*Silence.*)

JAMIE: I didn't know it was that bad.

EDWARD: Sometimes I think she's mad. And then, at other times . . . It's not simple, somehow.

JAMIE: She's not mad.

EDWARD: No, of course not. But you must admit she's not like most people.

JAMIE: Isn't that why you married her?

EDWARD: Yes, I suppose it is.

JAMIE: I sometimes wonder why you did marry her.

EDWARD: Well, really she married me.

JAMIE: But you must have wanted it.

EDWARD: Yes. Oh, yes. She was dazzling. She dazzled me. She was like a brilliant light. She made me see things I'd never seen. India! Nobody took their honeymoon in India back then. We saw the Taj Mahal together. It doesn't sound much now, but it was like a miracle to me. There I was, standing looking at the Taj Mahal by moonlight, with this dazzling girl beside me, holding my hand, reciting poetry by heart. She didn't know any poems about the Taj Mahal, so she recited "Ozymandias." "I met a traveller from an antique land . . ." I was so proud of her.

She could recite whole poems, on any subject, hundreds of them. It was like a trick, only it wasn't a trick, it was a passion. Alice taught me to love poetry. It rubbed off on me by sheer proximity. I've always been grateful for that.

JAMIE: I like it when you talk about the good times.

EDWARD: Yes, well . . .

(*Silence.*)

EDWARD: I'm going to leave.

(*Silence.*)

JAMIE: I knew it.

EDWARD: I'm sorry. I can't make Alice happy. I've tried, but I'm the wrong person. Also, ridiculous as it may sound, I've fallen in love.

JAMIE: What!

EDWARD: Yes. It's not what I expected, either.

JAMIE: Who is it?

EDWARD: Her name's Angela. She's the mother of a boy at school. He's been having problems, and I've been helping him.

JAMIE: Oh, God . . . Sorry, I didn't mean it like that. Only, what's going to happen to Ma?

EDWARD: I've given that a lot of thought. I've come to the conclusion that in the long run she'll be better off without me. I don't give her what she wants. I didn't realise it until I got to know Angela. With Angela, it's easy. The way I am seems to suit her. With Alice, everything I do is wrong. I'm nervous, and clumsy. I annoy her.

JAMIE: Does she know anything?

EDWARD: Not about Angela. No.

JAMIE: So it'll come out of nowhere?

EDWARD: Hardly nowhere. It's been getting worse and worse. Several times she's talked about separation.

JAMIE: She doesn't mean it.

EDWARD: Then why does she say it?

JAMIE: She feels there's something not real about her marriage.

EDWARD: Well, you see, she could be right.

JAMIE: I don't think she wants to be right.

EDWARD: That's why I was hoping you could stay on a bit.

JAMIE: Does it have to be today?

EDWARD: Well, it's what we've agreed. We've got everything ready.

JAMIE: Mightn't you change your mind?

EDWARD: No.

JAMIE: Once she sees you really might leave, she'll act differently with you.

EDWARD: I'm sorry. It's all gone too far.

JAMIE: Oh, God.

EDWARD: She'll still have you.

JAMIE: Look, I really don't know that I can do this.

EDWARD: I have to tell her soon.

JAMIE: What are you going to do? Move out?

EDWARD: Yes.

JAMIE: When?

EDWARD: Well, the plan was, soon. Very soon.

JAMIE: You don't mean today?

EDWARD: Angela felt, why drag it out?

JAMIE: You can't. You have to break it to her more gently.

EDWARD: Yesterday she asked me to say I loved her, and I couldn't speak the words. I can't go on like this.

JAMIE: Yes, but . . .

EDWARD: She'll be back from church soon. I'm going to tell her right away, and then I'm going to leave. You can be with her for a while, and still get off by four. You'll be in town by five-thirty. You don't have to go through Tunbridge Wells.

JAMIE: You planned this for when I was down.

EDWARD: Yes.

JAMIE: Have you packed a bag?

EDWARD: Just the basics.

JAMIE: So it's already happened.

EDWARD: Yes. It's just a matter of saying the words.

(*Silence.*)

JAMIE: How long will it take? I don't want to be here when you do it.

EDWARD: Give me half an hour.

JAMIE: I'll go for a walk, or something.

EDWARD: Right.

(*They both look at their watches, at the same time.*)

JAMIE: Half an hour, then.

EDWARD: Right.

(*Lights go down on* JAMIE.)

(EDWARD *finishes eating his breakfast.*)

(*Lights come up on* ALICE.)

ALICE: Jamie not up?

EDWARD: He's gone out for a walk.

ALICE: A walk? He never goes out for a walk.

EDWARD: Cup of tea?

(EDWARD *gets up and goes to make tea.* ALICE *sits at the breakfast table.*)

ALICE: Poor old Father Conlon produced a classic Connie sermon about women priests.

He said he couldn't make head or tail of the matter, but if the Pope says it's wrong then it's wrong, and that's why we're all in the Catholic Church. Wonderful.

EDWARD: What will you do about your printer?

ALICE: Try and get it fixed, I suppose.

EDWARD: You'd better buy yourself a new one.

ALICE: Edward, the money.

EDWARD: You can't do your anthology without one.

ALICE: Can we afford it?

EDWARD: I think we must, don't you?

ALICE: Maybe it could be my anniversary present.

EDWARD: If you like.

ALICE: After all, it is really for both of us. For your reports, and things. I promise not to drop it again.

EDWARD: Did the car start alright?

ALICE: Yes. First time.

EDWARD: It should go in for a service before the cold weather comes.

ALICE: I wonder what it is about going to mass. It's a dreary little building, really, and poor old Connie is such an ass. The language isn't beautiful any more. The congregation smells of wet socks. They all seem to wear nylon windcheaters these days, very bright colours, but somehow dismal.

The hymns are as hopeless as ever, as if the English Catholics got a job lot cheap when the Protties were throwing out the ones they no longer wanted. There's no sense of mystery any more, or the presence of God. And yet I always come away feeling better. Do you?

EDWARD: I think it's just one of those things I've got used to. I'm not sure I'd know what effect it was having unless I stopped.

ALICE: Maybe it's a sort of maintenance thing, like cleaning your teeth. Not very exciting in itself, but if you stop doing it your mouth tastes wrong.

EDWARD: Quite.

ALICE: Then of course whether you mean it or not you do say

things like, "Lord have mercy on us." I found myself counting. We asked for mercy seventeen times. Nine times in the Kyrie alone, of course. Three times in the Agnus Dei. And it kept popping up everywhere else. I think it may have a sort of hypnotic effect, all that asking for mercy. After a while it begins to strike you that maybe you need it.

EDWARD: Yes, I suppose we all do, really.

(*He brings over a mug of tea and puts it before* ALICE.)

ALICE: I'm sorry I hit you last night.

EDWARD: I expect it was my fault.

ALICE: I know I go for you sometimes. I'll try to stop. Really all I want is reassurance.

EDWARD: Right.

ALICE: Just to know that we're going through this thing together.

(*Silence.*)

After nearly thirty-three years.

(*Silence.*)

EDWARD: It's not really working, is it?

ALICE: What did you say?

EDWARD: It's not really working.

ALICE: Oh, thank God!

EDWARD: Why do you say that?

ALICE: That's the first time you've said it for yourself. I've been feeling as if it's only me, as if I'm going mad. But you do see it, don't you? We have to do something.

EDWARD: Yes. I see it.

ALICE: What's happened to us?

EDWARD: I think what you said is true. I've been walking away. I've been avoiding things.

ALICE: Oh, thank God! You're saying it at last!

EDWARD: I suppose I've felt I can't give you what you want. So I've felt like I'm not a very useful person, for you at least. I seem to annoy you, and do things wrong. That makes me feel, well, not much good, really, so I try not to talk about it. Which only makes it worse.

ALICE: Oh, thank God! You understand. I've been praying for this.

EDWARD: I think the truth is we're different kinds of people. It may just be that we don't work very well together.

ALICE: But we can! If we understand each other, and are real with each other, and if we have the will to make it work, then it'll work. I know it.

EDWARD: I'm not sure I have the will.

ALICE: You have to. Marriages only work because both people want them to work.

EDWARD: I'm not sure I want that.

ALICE: You're not sure you want our marriage to work?

EDWARD: I'm not sure.

ALICE: Edward, listen to me. This is terribly important. You must will our marriage, or it'll die. Do you understand that?

EDWARD: Yes.

ALICE: There's no in-between. It's either alive, or it's dead.

EDWARD: What if it's dead?

ALICE: Then we go our separate ways. No one can live in a dead marriage.

EDWARD: Maybe that's what we should do. Go. Our separate ways.

ALICE: But our marriage isn't dead.

EDWARD: Look at it, Alice. Look at us. Listen to us.

ALICE: Do you think it's dead?

(EDWARD *hesitates.* ALICE *answers for him.*)

Well, I don't. It's not dead for me. It's struggling to be born. It wants to breathe, and cry, and run about, and grow strong. It's our child, Edward, it's you and me, the best of you and me, the part that loves each other. All we have to do is give it a chance. So long as we love each other, we don't have to be afraid. I'm your wife. You're my husband. You see how simple it can be. You can say anything you want to me. Anything in the whole world.

(*Silence.*)

EDWARD: I want to leave.

ALICE: Leave?

EDWARD: Yes.

ALICE: Leave to go where?

EDWARD: There's someone else.

ALICE: Someone else?

EDWARD: I'm sorry.

(*Silence.*)

ALICE: How can there be someone else? What someone else?

EDWARD: A parent at school. You don't know her.

ALICE: What parent at school?

EDWARD: Her name's Angela Walker.

(*Silence.* ALICE *is struggling to take in what she's hearing.*)

I didn't mean it to happen. It was an accident. But it's happened.

ALICE: An accident? How was it an accident?

EDWARD: I met her to talk over her son's problems. She told me about the situation at home. The boy's father left a year or so ago. She became quite emotional. I said what I could. And that's how we—became close.

ALICE: Became close?

EDWARD: Yes.

ALICE: How close? No, I don't want to hear it. I can see it on your face. Oh, you traitor. You traitor. Was it as easy as that?

EDWARD: Yes.

ALICE: When did this "accident" happen?

EDWARD: About two months ago.

ALICE: And you went on just the same? I don't understand. Are you someone else?

EDWARD: I should have told you before—

ALICE: It's not an accident. You're doing it. You don't have to do it. You can stop doing it. You have to stop doing it.

EDWARD: I'm sorry. I can't.

ALICE: You're not free. Don't you realise that? This woman may have lost her husband, but that doesn't give her the right to take mine. Edward, this is ridiculous. You must see that. Or are you just doing this to give me a fright, and make me behave better?

EDWARD: No.

ALICE: Does Jamie know?

EDWARD: Some of it. I told him at breakfast.

ALICE: So he could console me?

EDWARD: Yes.

ALICE: You told Jamie?

EDWARD: I know this is all a shock. But I do truly think you'll come to see it's for the best.

ALICE: Of course I won't. What rot you talk.

EDWARD: I'm no good for you, Alice. I don't give you what you want.

ALICE: Of course not. You don't give me what I want because you're not even trying. You've found a way to sneak out of it. Well, you can't. I won't let you.

EDWARD: I'm sorry. I've made up my mind.

ALICE: Then you'll have to unmake it, won't you? This decision involves me. You have to consult me.

EDWARD: Don't do this, Alice. It'll only make it worse.

ALICE: You think I'm going to let you walk out of my life after thirty-three years because you can't be bothered to make an effort?

EDWARD: I have made an effort. For the last thirty-three years.

ALICE: What!

(*She starts to weep.*)

Don't say that. Not all of it. You don't mean that. Please, Eddie, don't take it all.

EDWARD: No, I don't mean that. But you know how it's been.

ALICE: We had India. You said you'd never forget India. We had those years when Jamie was little, in Maidstone. They were good years. Say they were good years, Edward.

45

EDWARD: Yes. They were good years.

ALICE: You mustn't take it all. You mustn't. You'll kill me.

EDWARD: I haven't forgotten India. When Jamie was little, they were good years.

(*Lights come up on* JAMIE.)

ALICE: Come here, darling.

(JAMIE *goes to her, and she takes him in her arms and rocks him as if he's a child.*)

Daddy says he wants to leave us.

(*She looks up at* EDWARD.)

Alright. You win. I'll do anything you say. You can have everything the way you want it. I won't go for you ever again. Just don't leave us.

EDWARD: You know it won't work.

ALICE: Yes, it will. I'll make it work.

EDWARD: Alice—

ALICE: It's all been my fault, Edward, I see that now, so now I want a chance to put things right. That's fair, isn't it? You owe me at least that. So just sit down and finish your breakfast.

EDWARD: I have finished.

(*But he sits down. Lights go down on* EDWARD.)

ALICE: Will he really leave? He won't, will he? Tell me he's just saying it to frighten me.

JAMIE: I think he'll leave.

ALICE: No! Tell me something else. It's no good, I can't take it. You have to tell me something else.

JAMIE: I'm sorry.

ALICE: What use is that to me?

JAMIE: I don't know what to say.

ALICE: Say it won't happen. Say there's something I can do to stop him leaving.

JAMIE: I don't know what to say.

ALICE: What's going to happen to me when I'm old?

(JAMIE *turns away.*)

What is it? Are you crying?

JAMIE: Sorry. I'll be alright in a minute.

ALICE: There, darling, there. Don't cry. Oh my darling, tell me what I'm to do and I'll do it for you. Please don't cry, my baby, my beloved, my beautiful boy. I'll pray for you and you pray for me, even if you don't believe the words you're saying, and the Lord will have mercy on us.

(*Lights go down on them.*)

(*Lights come up on* EDWARD. *He rises and steps forward.* JAMIE *also moves forward, to join him in the light.* ALICE *remains in darkness.*)

EDWARD: How is she?

JAMIE: Not good. I should have come down during the week. But this is a really busy time.

EDWARD: Angela thinks it's best that I stay away.

JAMIE: Have you phoned or anything?

EDWARD: No.

JAMIE: Right.

EDWARD: I've been thinking about the money side of things. I've decided I'm going to give her the house.

JAMIE: Oh, so she won't have to sell.

EDWARD: Angela's got her own house.

JAMIE: Right.

EDWARD: I think that's right, don't you?

JAMIE: Yes.

EDWARD: Does she know you're meeting me?

JAMIE: Yes. She's given me a message for you.

EDWARD: She wants me to come back.

JAMIE: Yes.

EDWARD: She's written to me at the school. Every day.

JAMIE: Every day? Five letters?

EDWARD: Well, four so far.

JAMIE: I'm to say you owe it to her to give her a chance. You did this out of the blue, without giving her warning or consulting her, and—well, there it is. I'm sure you know.

EDWARD: Out of the blue? What blue?

JAMIE: She wants you to go back, for a trial period, and if it doesn't work, then okay.

EDWARD: I can't. I've gone. I'm not coming back. She's got to understand that. I'll do everything I can to help, but I'm not coming back.

JAMIE: Right.

EDWARD: I'm sorry. I know that must sound hard. But it's a matter of survival. She'll never understand. She never did. I don't know who she thinks I am, but it's not me. Me is who I am with Angela. If I were to go back to Alice, it wouldn't be me going back.

JAMIE: Right.

EDWARD: Can you try to tell her that?

JAMIE: I don't think so.

EDWARD: Maybe it's not important. I just hate the way she says I'm taking the easy way out. Is wanting to come back to life taking the easy way out?

JAMIE: Right.

EDWARD: Sorry. It's hard enough for you as it is.

JAMIE: The thing is, I honestly don't know how she's going to get through this.

EDWARD: Both Angela and I think the less contact I have with her, the sooner she'll move on. No contact, in fact. Not directly. But that doesn't mean I won't do everything I can to help.

JAMIE: She's going to need time. She can't take it when you say it's all been decided. Without her.

EDWARD: I'll say anything she wants. I'll say black's white, if it makes any difference. But that part of my life is over. I'm not looking back.

JAMIE: That's the part I don't really understand.

EDWARD: What?

JAMIE: You seemed to care for her so much. And now . . . not.

(EDWARD *looks away.*)

EDWARD: Yes. It's not easy to explain.

(*Silence.*)

JAMIE: I'd better go back to her.

EDWARD: Right.

JAMIE: I'll be in touch.

EDWARD: Oh, I should have said. We've changed the phone number.

(*He takes out a pen and notebook and writes down a new number.*)

JAMIE: Does she call you?

EDWARD: She's called three times. Early morning every time.

JAMIE: What does she say?

EDWARD: Nothing.

JAMIE: Nothing? How do you know it's her?

EDWARD: I recognise the sound of her breathing.

JAMIE: You recognise—

(*He looks down. It's too much.*)

EDWARD: The new number. You won't—

JAMIE: No.

EDWARD: What if she asks you?

JAMIE: I'll say you won't give it out. I'm to leave messages at the school.

EDWARD: Fine.

JAMIE: I'd better get back.

(*A slight movement between them that might be the beginning of an embrace, or just a wave. The gestures die.*)

(*Lights go down on* EDWARD.)

(JAMIE *moves back into the room, as lights come up on* ALICE. *She's been waiting to hear the outcome of Jamie's meeting with Edward.*)

Do you want a cup of tea?

ALICE: Well?

(JAMIE *heads for the sink and proceeds to make tea.*)

JAMIE: I saw him.

ALICE: With her?

JAMIE: No. Just him.

ALICE: You can, you know. If you want.

JAMIE: I don't want.

ALICE: Did you tell him what I said?

JAMIE: Yes. He says he can't come back.

ALICE: Won't.

JAMIE: He says it's a matter of survival.

ALICE: What rot. That's his bloody retreat from Moscow. That's his big excuse. We're all going to die, but he can be one of the survivors if he doesn't have to drag me along too. It's his rotten stinking cowardly way of making out it's alright to dump me in the snow. But let me tell you, if we really were on the retreat from Moscow, he'd be the one who wouldn't make it, not me.

JAMIE: What's this?

(*He's found a scrap of paper in the cupboard.*)

ALICE: What does it look like?

JAMIE: (*Reading*) "I love you." What's it doing in the cupboard?

ALICE: And in the knife drawer. And by the phone message pad. And in the pocket of his gardening coat. And lots of places.

JAMIE: What for?

ALICE: Oh, I don't know. I suppose because while I was writing them, and hiding them in all the places where he might find them if he came back, it made me feel it could really happen. That he really would come back. And then when he found my notes, well—then he couldn't go away again.

(JAMIE *turns back to his tea making. It's hard for him.*)

So he told you he won't.

JAMIE: Yes.

ALICE: And what did you say to that?

JAMIE: What could I say?

ALICE: You could say, "You bastard. You murderer. You home-wrecker."

JAMIE: Well, I didn't.

ALICE: Why not? Do you think he's entitled to do what he's doing?

JAMIE: That's not for me to judge.

ALICE: Why not? If you saw a man beating a woman to death in the street, would you walk on by, saying, "That's not for me to judge?"

JAMIE: That's not how it is.

ALICE: This is a murder, Jamie. Just because there's no blood, don't think it's not a murder. He's murdering a marriage. Marriages don't bleed. But it's still murder.

JAMIE: I don't think it helps to talk like that.

ALICE: Oh? Well, tell me how to talk so it does help.

JAMIE: Marriages break down. It happens all the time. Nobody wants it to happen, but it does, and we have to live with it.

ALICE: It happens all the time, and we have to live with it? What sort of talk is that? Children are starving to death all the time, but it's not alright.

JAMIE: But we live with it.

ALICE: Not if it was my child. Not if it was you. If it was you starving to death, I'd let myself die first, to save you. Do you doubt that?

JAMIE: No.

ALICE: Well, this is my marriage. I'll do anything to save it.

JAMIE: I know that. But it's not my marriage.

(*Silence.*)

ALICE: You're like him. You just walk away.

JAMIE: I'm here, aren't I?

ALICE: But you want to walk away. You do, don't you?

(*Silence.*)

Go. I don't want you.

JAMIE: I can't.

ALICE: Why not? In case something happens to me, and you feel guilty?

JAMIE: Yes.

ALICE: Nothing's going to happen to me. That's what I can't bear. When you're alone, things stop happening.

JAMIE: Yes.

ALICE: I suppose you know about that.

JAMIE: Yes.

ALICE: How do you bear it?

JAMIE: Keep busy. Hope something will change sometime soon. Make the most of the little pleasures.

ALICE: What little pleasures?

JAMIE: Good food. Good books. Going to sleep with the radio on.

ALICE: Doesn't it keep you awake?

JAMIE: No. It sends you to sleep. Like being a child curled up on the sofa, while the grown-ups go on talking around you.

ALICE: Oh, darling. Is that what you want to be? The child curled up on the sofa?

JAMIE: Part of me.

ALICE: Were you happy when you were little? Did we give you a happy childhood? We did, didn't we?

JAMIE: Yes.

ALICE: He says it was a wrong turning in his life. But he can't go back like that. All those years really happened. How can he pretend they didn't?

JAMIE: I think that's just how he is. He lives in the present moment.

ALICE: I can't imagine that. I live in all the moments at once. My girlhood. School. The early days of our marriage. Yesterday. Now. They're all jostling about inside me, each one as vivid as the others. I dream about him, you know. I've dreamed about him every single night since he left. Quite friendly dreams, really. Then I wake.

(*She bows her head in pain.*)

JAMIE: I'm still here.

ALICE: No, you're not. You're in your flat. With your little pleasures.

JAMIE: You know what I mean. I'll always—you know.

ALICE: You'll always love me?

JAMIE: Yes.

ALICE: But even you can't say it. Already you start to be afraid. Better not say too much. No point in making promises you can't keep.

JAMIE: It's not a promise. It's just there. I'll always love you.

ALICE: Thank you for saying that, darling. But you have your own life to lead. Even I know that. I just have to manage as best as I can.

JAMIE: He told me he's decided you can have the house.

ALICE: Oh, has he? I suppose he thinks that makes everything alright.

JAMIE: I think he really does want to do what he can.

ALICE: So he told you I could have the house?

JAMIE: Yes.

ALICE: Well, he hasn't told me.

JAMIE: He wanted me to tell you.

ALICE: I don't care what he wanted. If he wants to make arrangements that affect me, he can come and talk to me himself. I won't have him using you as a messenger boy.

(*She goes to the phone and dials a number.*)

I can't stand the way he does it all without consulting me. That's odd. The line's making a funny noise.

JAMIE: He's changed the number.

ALICE: Changed the number?

JAMIE: He told me.

ALICE: So he's got a new number?

JAMIE: Yes.

ALICE: Have you got it?

JAMIE: No.

ALICE: Don't be silly, Jamie. Of course you have. I always could tell when you were lying.

JAMIE: I can't give it to you.

ALICE: Why not?

JAMIE: He asked me not to give it to you.

ALICE: Well, I ask you to give it to me.

JAMIE: I don't think it would help.

ALICE: That's not for you to judge, as you're so fond of saying. I'm grown-up. I'm not a criminal or a lunatic. I wish to be able to contact my husband.

JAMIE: I'll dial the number, and then you talk to him.

ALICE: It's starting already. I didn't know it would come so soon.

JAMIE: What?

ALICE: The pitying. The knowing looks. There she goes, she's one of them, you can't rely on them, they're desperate, they'll do anything—

JAMIE: Stop it.

ALICE: I think you'd better go.

JAMIE: Ma, please—

ALICE: Now. This minute. Before I do something embarrassing. Go on. Leave. It's what you want. You can't help. So why don't you just go?

JAMIE: I can't just leave you.

ALICE: Why not? You're no use to me. You've taken his side. You've left me already, just like he has. Well, if I'm to be alone, I'd rather be alone, and not have you dangling about pitying me, and patronising me. Go on! Leave! I don't have a husband any more, so I can't have a son, can I? It takes two to make a child, and there aren't two of us any more, so you don't exist!

JAMIE: Please don't do this—

ALICE: Do what? I've not done anything. I've not left him, he's left me. Go and tell him not to do this.

JAMIE: It won't change anything.

ALICE: You don't know that. Have you tried? You go on seeing him. That means you let him think he has your approval.

JAMIE: Ma, he's in love.

(*A terrible elongated cry of agony bursts from* ALICE.)

ALICE: No-o-o! No-o-o! Don't tell me that! Do you want to kill me? Oh God, oh God. What's going to happen to me when I'm old?

(*Lights go down on* ALICE.)

(*Very slowly, lights come up on* EDWARD, *as he speaks. At the same time, during the course of Edward's speech, the lights are fading on* JAMIE, *even as he listens to his father, carrying him away to a place from which he cannot respond.*)

EDWARD: Thirty-four years ago, I was standing on a platform at Charing Cross station, waiting to get on a train to Maidstone. I saw a man come walking down the platform who I thought was my father. I raised one arm and called, "Father!"—and with my arm still in the air, remembered that my father had died four months earlier. The man, a complete stranger, walked on by. The train came in. I got into a carriage. Another person got in, just we two in the carriage. The train left Charing Cross. The other person was a young woman. She was looking at me as if she was sorry for me. I realised there were tears on my cheeks. "What is it?" she said. "Oh, nothing," I said. "I mistook a man for my father, who's dead." And she said, "You must want to see him again very much." Now you should understand, this was true, but I hadn't known it. My father was a reserved man. I don't remember him ever embracing me. Somehow when this young woman, this stranger, said these words to me, I knew that all my life I'd wanted his embrace, and now it would never come. I began to weep. Continued weeping, I should say. And the young woman recited some lines from a poem I'd never heard, and have never forgotten since.

It is the only truth: it is the dream in us
That neither life nor death nor any other thing can take away:
But if she had not touched Him in the doorway of her dream

Could she have cared so much?
She was a sinner, we are but what we are:
The spirit afterwards, but first, the touch.

It's by Charlotte Mew, about Mary Magdalene, touching Jesus. How did that young woman in the train know what I was feeling? I was astounded. I felt as if I had stepped through a doorway into another world, where the inhabitants could read my heart. It was your mother, of course. It was Alice. And I was on the wrong train. It was the fast train, it never stopped at my station. We were almost at Dover before I realised it.

So you see, I made a mistake about Alice, right at the beginning, and she made a mistake about me. We thought we were like each other, and we weren't. I didn't know it. I did my best to be who she wanted me to be. And I suppose the real me went into hiding, like a—what do they call them? Terrorists who live ordinary lives for years and years, until the phone rings, and the order comes, Set off your bomb. Sleepers, they call them. Yes, I was a sleeper in my own marriage. All it took was Angela's hand on my arm. Her touch. I wept, like I wept on the train. Not for something I would never have. No, this time for gratitude. For the return of life. It was me she touched. Me. Me. No demands. No expectations. Just love.

How can I tell any of this to you, my son? My only child. Alice's child. How can I say to you that all those years ago, I got on the wrong train?

(*Lights out on* EDWARD, *and the stage is dark once more.*)

ACT TWO

JAMIE *enters, wearing a warm outdoor coat.*

JAMIE: Come on in.

(EDWARD *enters after him, also dressed for winter outdoors, and carrying a briefcase. He looks round.*)

EDWARD: I've always liked your flat. Does it still suit you?

JAMIE: It does the job.

(*They take off their coats, using similar movements.*)

EDWARD: Why do people have to have such big houses? One needs so little, really.

JAMIE: What can I get you? I have a bottle of New Zealand sauvignon open in the fridge.

(EDWARD *shakes his head, smiling.*)

EDWARD: New Zealand sauvignon . . .

JAMIE: It's good.

EDWARD: I'm sure it is. You have some. I'll just have a cup of tea.

JAMIE: Tea it is.

(*He goes to fill the kettle.*)

EDWARD: I belong to the tea-drinking generation. (*Looking round*) So you come back at the end of the day, and—what? Read the paper?

JAMIE: Have a bath, usually.

EDWARD: With the radio on?

JAMIE: Yes.

EDWARD: Six o'clock news?

JAMIE: If I'm lucky.

EDWARD: There's something inherently restful about the radio news. I don't know what it is.

JAMIE: Other people's problems.

EDWARD: Why should that be restful?

JAMIE: Knowing other people's lives go wrong too. One doesn't feel so left out.

EDWARD: Maybe that's it. Well, I won't stay long. Then you can have your bath.

JAMIE: No hurry.

(EDWARD *takes a letter out of his pocket.*)

EDWARD: Alice wants me to go to the house. To sign the papers.

JAMIE: Yes. She told me.

EDWARD: I think it's a mistake. So does Angela.

JAMIE: I think she's pretty set on it.

EDWARD: If she makes a scene, I shall just leave. I won't be drawn in, Jamie. There's no point.

JAMIE: She says she'll behave herself.

(EDWARD *hands him the letter.*)

EDWARD: I think you should read that.

(JAMIE *reads the letter.*)

What do you think?

JAMIE: Well . . . It doesn't surprise me. It's how she talks.

EDWARD: Do you think I should take it seriously?

(JAMIE *gives back the letter as the kettle boils. He makes tea.*)

JAMIE: How do you mean, seriously?

EDWARD: Well—(*reading*) "You have committed a murder, but no one believes it. All that I can do now is kill myself, then everyone will see what you have done."

JAMIE: I don't know, Pa. What do you want me to say?

EDWARD: Do you think she'd do it?

JAMIE: No. Maybe. I don't know. Would it change anything if I said yes?

EDWARD: No. I don't think it would.

JAMIE: Well, then.

EDWARD: Does that sound cruel to you?

JAMIE: I don't know. I don't know. All this is . . . I'm finding it quite hard, actually.

(*He gives his father the mug of tea.* EDWARD *sips as he speaks.*)

EDWARD: The plain fact is, Alice has been accustomed to getting her own way with me—which is my fault, I freely admit it—and she can't accept, just can't accept, that I'm not still—in her power. This letter is a power play, it's blackmail, it's an act of aggression, directed straight at me, and if I give in to it—you must see that I can't. What kind of life would it be, for her as well as me, if I went back because of this?

JAMIE: Yes, I do see that. But I see how she is, too. She's just so . . . sad.

EDWARD: Well, there's that too, of course.

JAMIE: What would you do, if . . .

EDWARD: What could I do? It would be too late.

(*Their eyes meet: sharing the same guilty thought.*)

JAMIE: Yes.

EDWARD: How was she when you last saw her?

JAMIE: Very low. It wasn't easy to leave.

EDWARD: When was that? Sunday?

JAMIE: Yes. I'm going down every weekend at present.

EDWARD: I'm very grateful to you, Jamie. And very sorry this burden has to fall on you.

JAMIE: So you will come? To sign the papers?

EDWARD: Yes. I'll come. But it'll be the last time. Tell her, if you can. The last time.

(*They both sit, in the armchairs.*)

(*Lights go down on* EDWARD.)

(JAMIE *picks up a Sunday newspaper and settles down to reading it.*)

(*Far off, the sound of a bugler playing "The Last Post."*)

(ALICE *speaks, as if offstage, to an unseen puppy.*)

ALICE: Stay! Stay, Eddie! Good boy.

(*She enters, just back from church. She wears a long loose coat.* JAMIE *gets up to investigate, and sees the puppy, outside the back door.*)

JAMIE: Hello. Who are you?

ALICE: He arrived on Wednesday.

JAMIE: Well, well. You're a friendly one, aren't you? What's your—

(*He turns round, just as* ALICE *is removing her coat, to reveal that she's wearing a multicoloured pajama suit.*)

Good God! What are you wearing?

ALICE: I went up to London, to the Designer Sale. It was only twenty-five pounds. Do you like it?

JAMIE: Well, yes. But it makes you look like a clown.

ALICE: That's alright, then. Clowns are happy people. Don't you love him? He's so affectionate. He does me more good than all my tranquilisers.

JAMIE: What's his name?

ALICE: Eddie. He's not fully house-trained yet, so he has to stay outside until he's done his duty. Don't you, my darling?

JAMIE: He can't be called Eddie.

ALICE: Well, he's called Edward, really.

JAMIE: Ma, you can't do this.

ALICE: Why not? I can do anything I like.

JAMIE: It's just—well, it's such a giveaway.

ALICE: What does it give away? Look, I'm training him.

(*She points a commanding finger at the offstage puppy.*)

Stay, Edward! Stay!

JAMIE: Oh, Ma. It's embarrassing.

ALICE: I don't see why. I'm not embarrassed. Why should you be embarrassed?

(*Their eyes track the puppy as it wanders off.*)

JAMIE: He doesn't even stay when you tell him to.

ALICE: I'm training him. He'll learn. You stay out there till you've done your duty, Eddie!

JAMIE: Can't you call him Fido, or something? No, not Fido.

ALICE: Everyone says, "Poor Alice, her husband's left her, now she'll get a pet." Fine. Now I've got a pet. And as a matter of fact he's better than Edward in every respect but two. One is, he won't live as long. And the other I'm not telling you.

JAMIE: Well, he's very sweet, whatever he's called.

ALICE: He's a darling.

JAMIE: So is this meeting supposed to be lunch, or after lunch?

ALICE: What lunch?

JAMIE: It's almost one o'clock. That normally means lunch.

ALICE: Normality has been suspended.

JAMIE: Oh. So no lunch.

ALICE: I expect there's something in the fridge, if you're hungry.

JAMIE: What about you?

ALICE: I don't bother with eating any more. It's cheaper, and it saves an amazing amount of time.

JAMIE: You have to eat. You don't want to starve to death.

ALICE: Yes I do.

JAMIE: You don't look as if you're starving to death.

ALICE: Yes, well, I keep forgetting. I'm thinking about this or that, and I find I've eaten a tin of baked beans without noticing.

JAMIE: Do you open the can without noticing?

ALICE: I suppose I must. Did I tell you why I was so late back from church?

JAMIE: No.

ALICE: Traffic. You wouldn't believe the number of cars there are on the roads on a Sunday. And do you know why that is?

JAMIE: Why?

ALICE: It's all the husbands who've left their wives. They're all going back to their families for their Sunday visit.

(JAMIE *laughs.*)

You think I'm joking, but I'm not. Every time a marriage breaks down, you get more cars on the roads. Half of all marriages now end in divorce, you know. That's millions and millions of extra car journeys. No wonder there's global warming.

JAMIE: So don't leave your wife, or the world will end.

ALICE: Exactly.

JAMIE: I must say, you seem to be coping a bit better.

ALICE: Do I?

JAMIE: Have you gone back to the anthology?

ALICE: Oh, no. I'm not doing that any more.

JAMIE: That's a pity. I thought it sounded good.

ALICE: No, you didn't. You thought it gave me something to do.

JAMIE: Well, we all need something to do. No disgrace in that.

ALICE: You don't really have any idea, do you?

JAMIE: Any idea of what?

ALICE: What it's like to be a left woman.

JAMIE: No, I suppose I don't.

ALICE: It's not just the loneliness. It's being poorer. It's not being respected by other people. It's being pitied and avoided. It's going to church more than you used to. It's watching TV more than you used to. It's waking up in the morning and not bothering to dress, because there's no one to see. It's making a meal and not eating it, because there's no one to eat it with. It's not doing your hair or your face, because there's no one to look nice for. It's getting a pet and loving it too much. It's slowly feeling yourself turn into a batty old crone who talks to herself. And the worst of it is, you don't die. Like Moscow— the glorious end of the great march—only it's empty. So you have to turn around, and start the long march home. It's winter. You're freezing. Starving. You just want to lie down in the snow and die. And all the time you know you're not going somewhere, you're leaving somewhere. You're on the retreat.

(*She goes to the fridge.*)

That's how it is for me. How is it for you?

JAMIE: Much the same as ever, I suppose.

ALICE: How's your love life?

JAMIE: Private.

ALICE: So you're still on your own. There's bread, ham, and half a cucumber. We won't die today. I wonder why you haven't found anyone. You look perfectly normal.

JAMIE: I'd rather you kept out of my private life, really.

ALICE: Yes, I know. But it involves me too.

JAMIE: How?

ALICE: Well, if you're no good at making people love you, that's my fault, isn't it? Or Edward's fault, for being such a sneaking snivelling excuse for a man.

JAMIE: I wish you wouldn't say things like that. He's still my father. I still love him.

ALICE: So what? So do I.

(*She puts out food for lunch.*)

It was the Remembrance Day service today. We joined in with the Protties at the parish church. It's very moving, you know. "At the going down of the sun," and so forth. "They shall not grow old, as we grow old." There was a Boy Scout band, with a little bugler playing "The Last Post." I found myself thinking about the two wars, and the wives and mothers waiting at home, and the telegrams from the War Office that told them their husbands and sons were dead. I thought of how terrible that must have been, and yet somehow easier to bear than losing Edward the way I've lost him. And then all at once I saw it. This is our war. This is what makes widows and orphans nowadays. Only, there aren't any graves, or Remembrance Day services. And we're not allowed to mourn.

(*She sits down at the table and starts to eat absent-mindedly.*)

So you see, I'm not really coping after all. I keep thinking of "Dover Beach." "Ah love, let us be true to one another." Matthew Arnold saw the horror. How the world is so full of hurt and wrong that we just mustn't add to it. Oh, Jamie, I want so much to go to Edward and say, "You mustn't do this, it's wrong, it's part of the cruelty we have to fight every day, every minute."

(*As she speaks the lines of Arnold's poem,* EDWARD *rises from his chair, still in darkness, draws on his overcoat, and picks up his briefcase. He moves round past her, to take up a position from which he can "enter" once more.*)

Ah, love, let us be true
To one another! for the world, which seems
To lie before us like a land of dreams,
So various, so beautiful, so new,
Hath really neither joy, nor love, nor light,
Nor certitude, nor peace, nor help for pain . . .

(EDWARD *is heard offstage, reacting to the puppy.*)

EDWARD: Who are you? Where have you come from?

(*Lights come up on* EDWARD *as he enters, visibly ill at ease, briefcase in one hand.*)

(*He steps in dog mess.*)

Oh, God!

(*He goes back out to clean the underside of his shoe.*)

Oh, Lord! Where did that come from?

ALICE: Edward! Good boy!

EDWARD: What?

ALICE: Not you. Good boy, Eddie! You've done your duty.

(EDWARD *comes in again, now even more nervous.*)

JAMIE: Hello, Pa.

EDWARD: Hello, Jamie. Thanks for coming.

JAMIE: No problem.

ALICE: Hello. I'm here too. Hello, hello, hello.

EDWARD: How are you, Alice?

ALICE: Fine. Fine. Fine.

EDWARD: I didn't know you'd got a dog.

ALICE: He's new. Jamie thinks he's some kind of substitute for you. I can't think why.

(EDWARD *joins them at the table, and puts down his briefcase.*)

EDWARD: I still think we should have left it to the solicitor to do this.

ALICE: Well, I don't.

EDWARD: Just to make sure it's all done properly, I mean.

ALICE: If you'd left the solicitors to do it, it might have been done legally, but it wouldn't have been done properly.

JAMIE: Ma. You promised.

ALICE: Yes, alright. I'll behave myself. I'll be a good girl.

(EDWARD *takes out various papers.*)

EDWARD: This is the deed signing over the house in your sole name. This is the summary of the financial agreement. This is the application for the decree. Everything's exactly the way I explained it to Jamie. All we have to do is sign.

ALICE: What happens if I don't?

EDWARD: Well, this agreement lapses, I suppose. And we start again. But I have to say, in your interest, that this is a very good settlement. No court would give half as much. You get the entire value of the family home—

ALICE: Stop it.

(*Silence.*)

I'm sorry. How can you sit there and say I get the entire value of the family home, when the entire value of the family home is precisely what you've taken from me?

EDWARD: I knew this wouldn't work.

ALICE: Yes. It will. Look, I'm being businesslike. No more references to sneaking, two-faced marital treachery. So tell me, Edward. This settlement of yours. Do I get more than I would get if you died?

EDWARD: If I died? Well, no. As things stand, if I died, you'd get the house, our savings, and a full widow's pension.

ALICE: And if we get a divorce, I get less?

EDWARD: Well, yes. I mean, if I'm still alive, I have to have something, don't I?

ALICE: So it would be better for me if you were dead.

EDWARD: Perhaps. But I'm not.

ALICE: It would be better in every way. If I have to manage without you, I'd rather be a widow. A widow has so much more status than a left woman. I could put flowers on your grave, and remember all the good times we had, and look forward to being with you again in heaven, "reunited," as they put on the gravestones—

JAMIE: Ma—

ALICE: Only as things stand, there's no grave, and you've poisoned all my memories, and when we meet again in the next world, there'll be bloody Angela clogging the place up.

(EDWARD *half rises.*)

EDWARD: I shouldn't have agreed to this. Angela was right.

ALICE: Fuck Angela! There, I said a disgusting word. I apologise. But you make me do these things, Edward, really you do. It's the way you walk away. It drives me mad.

EDWARD: Is there any point in going on with this?

ALICE: Is there any point? Yes, there's a point. Look at Jamie. He's our son. He's part you and part me. We made him. We joined together, and we made him. Don't you feel how sacred that is? You know as well as I do that the Church says marriage is a bond that can't be dissolved. And that's why. It makes people. You can get lawyers to put whatever you want on paper, but you're still my husband and Jamie's father, and you will be till the day you die.

EDWARD: I know your view—

ALICE: This isn't a view. This is how it is.

EDWARD: For you.

ALICE: No, not just for me. For everybody. You can't invent a private reality.

EDWARD: Nor can you.

ALICE: Mine isn't a private reality.

EDWARD: Well then, nor's mine.

ALICE: Yes it is. Isn't it, Jamie?

JAMIE: Don't ask me to take sides.

ALICE: Don't ask you to take sides? Between reality and madness? That's what it is, deciding when you're married and when you're not, whenever it happens to suit you. It's madness and chaos.

(EDWARD *starts to put the papers back in his briefcase.*)

What are you doing?

EDWARD: Are you going to sign the papers?

ALICE: I don't see why I should.

EDWARD: So I might as well go.

JAMIE: Ma, you're making a mistake.

ALICE: Am I, darling? Tell me what I should do.

JAMIE: Sign the papers. It's a very generous settlement.

ALICE: You still don't see it, do you? I don't care about money. I care about love. I love you, Edward, whether I want to or not. We're bound up together. I never thought in a million years that you'd stop loving me. How could you? You were my husband. Now that I know, I'll behave differently, if you'll only help me a little. I don't need much. Just tell me you do love me, for all my stupidity and blindness, and you'll see, I'll be a good wife, and a loving wife, and I'll make you happy.

(*Silence.*)

EDWARD: What do I have to do or say to get it through to you once and for all that I've gone?

(*Lights go down on* EDWARD.)

(JAMIE *sits with bowed head.*)

ALICE: So is it all over for me?

JAMIE: Ma—

ALICE: Be very careful what you say, Jamie. I have so little left, I hardly know how to crawl from one minute to the next. The future is quite blank. No looking forward. No hope. No expectation of happiness. But that doesn't matter. Almighty God isn't interested in our happiness, only in our salvation. Say a prayer with me, Jamie. I'm not saying you have to believe in the teachings of the Church. Or the Bible. It's just an act of humility, really. It's saying, "I don't understand. I get things wrong. But I can be forgiven." Please, darling. Say my prayer with me. All it's saying is, "I'm part of something so much bigger than me." It's saying, "I don't control my own life." It's such a small prayer, but it makes living bearable.

JAMIE: You believe enough for both of us. You don't need me to believe too.

ALICE: I know. But as a favour to me. It's only words.

JAMIE: What do you want me to say?

ALICE: Lord, have mercy on us.

JAMIE: Lord, have mercy on us.

ALICE: Thank you.

(JAMIE *rises, and walks away.*)

(*Lights go down on* ALICE *and* JAMIE.)

(*Lights come up on* EDWARD.)

EDWARD: Was I too cruel? I have to make her accept what's happened, for her own good. It's not like me to be cruel. I was brought up to think of others. My father would say, "You're not the only pebble on the beach." I grew up knowing it without ever thinking about it. I was a pebble, like the millions of other pebbles. What claim has a pebble on the attention of the world? When I think about it now, I want to say, "Am I less of a pebble than all the others? Do I deserve less? Are their needs to come before mine?" But all this is very recent. I handle these feelings clumsily. I don't mean to be cruel. Alice said to me, again and again, "Tell me what you want." She never understood. I was brought up not to want things. Not for myself. So after a while you—forget . . .

(*Now lights begin to come up once more on* JAMIE.)

Did I ever tell you, my first ambition was to be an archaeologist? When I was a boy I read about Howard Carter finding the tomb of Tutankhamen. I was so excited I lay awake all night. It wasn't the treasure that thrilled me. It was the pure act of discovery. To push through that last crumbling tunnel wall, to feel the rush of stale air on your face, to hold up a lamp in the darkness and see—wonders! That was how I came to love the past. I try to remember that, when I'm teaching. How it all started with a sense of wonder. (*Pause*) I never meant to be cruel.

JAMIE: It's alright. I know. It's just that I don't know how to help her.

EDWARD: Yes. I'm sorry.

JAMIE: I find it harder every time. Going home.

EDWARD: Perhaps you should tell her.

JAMIE: How can I tell her? I'm all she's got.

EDWARD: Yes, I do see that.

JAMIE: Last weekend I found her sitting in the same chair in the same position as when I'd left her. It was like she hadn't moved for a week. Like her life stops until I come home again. But I have a life too.

EDWARD: Of course you do. You have to think of yourself too. She must understand that.

JAMIE: How can I think of myself when she's falling apart?

(*Pause.*)

EDWARD: Perhaps there's some way you could ask her to help you.

JAMIE: Me? I'm alright.

EDWARD: Just to get her out of herself.

JAMIE: Oh. Yes. I see.

EDWARD: Anyway. Just a thought.

(*Lights go down on* EDWARD. JAMIE *sits, hunched in his own thoughts.*)

(*Lights come up on* ALICE. *She watches him in silence for a moment.*)

ALICE: Are you alright, darling?

JAMIE: Yes, I'm fine. Why wouldn't I be?

ALICE: Don't sound so surprised. You're allowed to have things go wrong too.

JAMIE: Nothing's going wrong. It's just that things are getting a bit hectic at work these days.

ALICE: Ah.

JAMIE: It gives me a few problems.

ALICE: Yes, I see. So you may not be able to come down for a while.

JAMIE: Well, maybe not quite so often. Once a month, maybe. Do you mind?

ALICE: No, darling. I'll manage.

JAMIE: I'm trying to be the good son. But I'm not as good at it as I thought.

(*She kisses him.*)

ALICE: You are. More than I deserve. I know I must be very wearing.

JAMIE: Well, to be honest—the way things are at present—I can't take it for too long at a time.

ALICE: I can't take it for too long at a time either.

(*A shared look of amused sympathy.* JAMIE *feels relieved.*)

JAMIE: Actually, there are one or two things going wrong for me, in a minor sort of way.

ALICE: Is it work? Or the other thing?

JAMIE: The other thing.

ALICE: Why?

JAMIE: It's what you said. It seems I'm not very good at making people love me.

ALICE: How could anyone not love you?

JAMIE: I think I'm a bit unforthcoming.

ALICE: Like Edward.

JAMIE: Probably.

ALICE: You must get over it, darling. You must forthcome.

JAMIE: It doesn't seem to be easy.

ALICE: But you do want to?

JAMIE: Oh, I want all the usual things. Only, it doesn't happen. There was someone. But then she decided it wasn't working out for her. I'm not quite sure why. It seems I'm the problem.

ALICE: Like me.

JAMIE: I'm sorry. I shouldn't be talking about myself.

ALICE: It makes a change.

JAMIE: Why are you looking at me like that?

ALICE: I'm trying to think how I can help you.

JAMIE: Oh, I'll be alright.

ALICE: I want to say to you, "Pray about it." But I suppose you won't. Would you mind if I prayed for you?

JAMIE: No.

ALICE: If it works, will you start believing again?

JAMIE: If it doesn't, will you stop?

ALICE: I couldn't even if I wanted to. Which I do. If I could only stop believing, then I could get out. Which I long to do, night and day.

JAMIE: Get out?

ALICE: Lie down in the snow and fall asleep. No more waking. The waking hurts so much. That moment, coming out of a confusion of dreams, when you say, "Maybe it's not true after all. Maybe he's lying there, beside me." And the dreams fade away, and you turn your head on the pillow, and there's no one there. So you see, every night when I go to bed I pray to Almighty God, "Take me tonight. Don't leave me to morning, to wake alone."

JAMIE: I know I should say, "Come and live with me." But I can't.

ALICE: It's alright, darling. I don't want to.

JAMIE: I think I'm just too frightened.

ALICE: Of my unhappiness.

JAMIE: Yes.

ALICE: It frightens me, too.

JAMIE: But you wouldn't, would you? Lie down in the snow.

ALICE: I can't make any promises.

JAMIE: No, but you wouldn't. You've lasted this far.

ALICE: This far, and now where? When Edward was here—that was my last shot. You heard him.

JAMIE: Just tell me you wouldn't do anything stupid.

ALICE: I've been doing stupid things all my life.

JAMIE: But not that.

ALICE: Why not? I'm sunk. I'm done for. I want to get out. What is there to wait around for? Do you think it's going to get any better?

JAMIE: People get used to things.

ALICE: Maybe. But what for? Just tell me that.

JAMIE: I can't.

ALICE: So there it is, you see.

(*Silence.*)

JAMIE: If you did—what would you do?

ALICE: I don't know. It doesn't much matter to me.

JAMIE: It does to me. I'm the one who'd have to clear up afterwards.

ALICE: Yes, I suppose so. I'll try not to make a mess.

JAMIE: I shouldn't have said that. That's not what matters at all.

ALICE: It's alright, darling.

JAMIE: No, I want to say something different. I want to show you I do understand. After all, suppose it was cancer, and you were in unbearable pain, and dying, only too slowly. I'd say, "End it now," wouldn't I? Out of my love for you. So if your life hurts you so much you want to end it, I won't stop you. Out of my love for you. Only, tell me. Don't let it be a surprise. Give me time to say good-bye.

ALICE: My darling boy. How you've grown up. You must have known some sad dark times to say that to me.

JAMIE: I have. I do.

ALICE: I'll tell you before I do anything. I promise.

JAMIE: And there's something else I want to say. I can't ask you to live for me. We each have to carry our own burden. But you're like the explorer. You're further down the road. You've gone on ahead. So if after a while you don't go on any more, I'll know the road is too hard, for too long. I'll know that in the end the unhappiness wins. But if you do go on, and bear it, terrible as it is, then I'll know that however bad it gets, I can last it out. Because you did, before me.

(*Lights go down on* ALICE.)

(*Lights come up on* EDWARD.)

EDWARD: When you read the diaries written by the men on the retreat, there's one question that comes up again and again. Is it my duty to save my comrade's life, even at the risk of losing my own? Or am I permitted, am I entitled, to do what is necessary for my own survival?

(JAMIE *turns, almost reluctantly, to listen to him.*)

It's called survivor guilt. Not really a rational emotion at all. We're not talking about killing others so that you can live. We're talking about a situation where either everyone dies, or by abandoning the weak, the strong survive. I know it seems brutal. But what's the point of everyone ending up dead?

JAMIE: It doesn't seem brutal, so much as convenient.

EDWARD: Maybe it is. Alice has started sending me packages, you know. Full of newspaper cuttings about suicides and murders, with notes that say, "Now you're part of all this." She sends them to the school, and doesn't put "Personal" on the outside, so the school secretary opens them. I wish she wouldn't do that. This is our own private business, after all.

JAMIE: She doesn't feel that. She feels this is part of something much bigger. Like a war. And she's one of the casualties.

EDWARD: And I'm the enemy.

JAMIE: No, you're the traitor. The friend who turned out to be an enemy.

EDWARD: The traitor! I've always thought of myself as a good person. Almost too good for my own good, if you see what I mean. And now Alice has cornered all the suffering, and suddenly I'm the bad one. All those years of Alice going for me, and not listening, not wanting to know, laughing at my habits, rubbishing my tastes—I don't know anything about wine, why did she make me take her out to smart restaurants and order wine, and then get cross with me because I didn't know how to? I mean, what was the point of that? And the crossword. You know I love to do the crossword. I don't know why, I've no doubt it's very boring of me, but I find it settles me. Why did she have to sneer at it, and go on at me as soon as I'd sat down with it, and make me do jobs that could perfectly easily wait half an hour? Why couldn't she say, "He's had a hard day in school, he loves his crossword, let him do it in peace?"

JAMIE: She thought it was one of your ways of avoiding her.

EDWARD: Well, I expect it was. But why did I want to avoid her? Because I always felt criticised by her. That's true, you know. Right from the very beginning, I was always afraid that I was saying or doing the wrong thing. Most of all saying. I don't always put things very well, and when I see that look on her face that says, "Well? Get on with it. I'm listening," my thoughts get muddled up, and I can hear myself talking nonsense. So I just stop. And she says, "Can't you even talk now?" I hate that. I really hate it. You'd have hated it, Jamie. You would.

JAMIE: I would. I did.

EDWARD: So. There you are.

(*Pause.*)

The way it was before, I felt everything I did was wrong—but I was innocent. Now, I feel that what I'm doing is right—but I feel guilty.

JAMIE: Because you survived.

EDWARD: Yes.

(*Pause.*)

I've decided to take early retirement. I'm unlikely to get another position at my age. Durham, we thought.

JAMIE: Durham! Why do you have to go so far away?

EDWARD: It's where Angela comes from. She has family up there. She can sell her house. We should be alright.

JAMIE: Yes, I expect you will be.

EDWARD: Really, I should have left years ago.

JAMIE: Why didn't you?

EDWARD: You don't let yourself think things. It never really seemed an option.

JAMIE: Why not? You knew you weren't happy. Even I knew you weren't happy.

EDWARD: And Alice. She wasn't happy. She knew we weren't right for each other.

JAMIE: No. She didn't. Right up to the day you left she thought you adored her.

EDWARD: How could she think that?

JAMIE: Because you went on being nice, and making cups of tea, and acting like you were happy. Because you never got angry when she went for you. Because you never told her what you wanted, or what it felt like to be you. You just went on pretending—and pretending—and one day—you left. If I were to blame you for anything, it would be that.

EDWARD: I know.

(*Pause.*)

JAMIE: So—it's going alright? With Angela?

EDWARD: Yes. Yes. It's good.

JAMIE: Does she let you do the crossword?

EDWARD: Oh, yes. I get home at the end of the day, and we have a cup of tea, and I settle down with the crossword. If I'm stuck on a clue, I try it out on her. Quite often she gets it, right away. If she doesn't get it right away, I'd say she tends not to get it ever. Whereas I work more methodically, by elimination, and I usually get there in the end.

JAMIE: The pure act of discovery.

EDWARD: Does it all sound to you like a ridiculous existence?

JAMIE: No. No more so than any of the rest of us.

(*Lights go down on* EDWARD.)

(*Lights come up on* ALICE.)

ALICE: I've joined a new group, called the Lighthouse Keepers. I'm on a rota. Every few days I go to the office and answer the phones. It's a help-line, and it's for people who think they've got AIDS, or want to know about AIDS, or want information about treatment. There's always two other people on the phones with me, and a supervisor, and when the phones aren't ringing, we chat to each other. And you know what I've discovered? Homosexuals are the kindest people.

JAMIE: What did you think they were like?

ALICE: I've never really thought anything about them at all. I've not been prejudiced against them, of course. But I had no idea they were so nice. They're terribly sweet to me. It makes me want to be a homosexual, only I'm not sure how one goes about it.

JAMIE: What on earth do you know about AIDS?

ALICE: Nothing at all, darling. There's a fact sheet for all that.

JAMIE: So what do you say to the people who phone up?

ALICE: Well, we talk about this and that. They tell me about their boyfriends, you know. And nearly every time it turns out they've been left, just like me. So we talk about what it's like, and how men are all selfish pigs, and how is one to cope. I recite lines from poems to them—

JAMIE: Poems?

ALICE: I tell them about God—

JAMIE: Poems and God?

ALICE: Both together, sometimes. Like those marvellous lines of Rilke's—

> *A sensation of falling is not unique or new.*
> *My failing falling hand*
> *Has got the falling sickness even Caesar*
> *Could not withstand.*
> *Yet underneath I know another hand*
> *A falling universe cannot fall through.*

JAMIE: What do the others on the help-line make of all this?

ALICE: They were a bit flummoxed to start with, but we got talking, and oh, Jamie, they're so loving. I think I've found out why. It's not that homosexuals are really any better than the rest of us, in themselves, but the prejudice against them, and now this terrifying disease, makes them aware of suffering, it puts them on the side of people in pain. I can't tell you how sweet they are to me.

JAMIE: Do any of them actually have AIDS?

ALICE: Oh, yes. Several of them are HIV Positive. That's what you say. You don't say they've got AIDS. Oh, and I've told them all about you, and they all agree you're probably gay.

JAMIE: Well, I'm not, as it happens.

ALICE: Why not? Are you prejudiced?

JAMIE: No. Not at all.

ALICE: You could be refusing to admit your true nature.

JAMIE: Do you want me to be gay?

ALICE: It would rather lessen the chances of grandchildren. Did you see Edward?

JAMIE: Yes.

ALICE: What was it all about?

JAMIE: He wants to move. To Durham.

ALICE: So he doesn't have to meet me in Tesco?

JAMIE: Pretty much.

ALICE: He's such a coward.

(*She hears the sound of a dog yapping offstage.*)

Did I tell you? I've taught Eddie a trick.

(*She goes to the back door to look for the puppy in the garden.*)

Eddie! Stop running round in circles for one minute. Eddie!

Show Uncle Jamie your trick. Sit! Watch this, Jamie. Die, Edward! Die!

(JAMIE *watches, shaking his head.*)

There. Isn't he clever?

JAMIE: Yes.

ALICE: Wouldn't it be something if I could do that with the real Edward?

JAMIE: Make him die?

ALICE: Well, roll about on the floor a bit.

(*She watches fondly as the dog reverts to racing about the garden.*)

JAMIE: Oh, well. I suppose it's an improvement on the way you were talking a few weeks ago.

ALICE: What was I saying a few weeks ago?

JAMIE: About lying down in the snow.

ALICE: Oh, that. Yes, I've moved on from that. I have a much better plan.

JAMIE: I'm relieved to hear it.

ALICE: The thing about unhappiness is, after a while it stops being interesting. So you have to do something different.

Now I shall have to get on with it sooner than I'd expected. I'm not driving all the way to Durham.

JAMIE: What exactly is this much better plan?

ALICE: Did I tell you I'd gone back to my anthology?

JAMIE: No.

(*She picks up a file to show him.*)

ALICE: In fact, I've finished it. It's all done, and I have all the pages in a file, loose, but in the correct order.

JAMIE: That's wonderful.

ALICE: Darling, putting pages in order requires very little skill.

JAMIE: I'm just glad you've actually finished it.

ALICE: So this is my plan. I take my anthology, and inside it, between Lost Love and The Long March Home, which is the last section, I place a kitchen knife.

(*She draws a knife out of the file, shows it to him, and puts it back.*)

JAMIE: For heaven's sake!

ALICE: I go to the love nest. I ring the front door bell. Edward opens the door. I march into the living room. Edward follows me, bleating and stammering. That other woman—I don't have a clear picture of her, I'm not sure where she is, but she's not there. She's gone out. I say to Edward, "I want you to come home." He says he can't. Never won't, always can't. I show him the file. "Look," I say, "my anthology, it's finished." He bleats and stammers some more. "I want you to have it," I say. "Since you've taken everything else I ever loved." I hold it out to him.

(*She holds the file out.*)

He doesn't take it. He—I don't know what he does. It doesn't really matter. Then I take out the knife—

(*She takes out the knife, very quickly, making* JAMIE *jump.*)

That frightens him. I say, "Since you won't come home, I'm going to kill myself." Then holding the knife very firmly, I slash my left wrist—

(*She half-makes the gesture, causing* JAMIE *to leap forward in alarm.*)

JAMIE: Don't!

ALICE: Severing the artery, and spurting blood all over the room. Whoosh-whoosh-whoosh-whoosh!

(*She waves her arm around as if it's a hosepipe run out of control.*)

JAMIE: For God's sake!

ALICE: Edward's not at all competent when things get messy. By the time he's stopped flapping about, I'll have bled to death. Then he'll be sorry. And she'll come home and find blood all over her fitted carpet.

JAMIE: Please put that knife away.

ALICE: Yes, I should. I sharpened it for half an hour the other day. It's like a razor.

(*She puts the knife back into the file.*)

JAMIE: You really scare me, waving that thing around.

ALICE: Do I? You know something really interesting I've learned? When you feel powerless, you become strongly attracted to violence. It's a shortcut to power. Obvious really, but I'd never quite seen it before.

JAMIE: You could have an accident, you know. Playing with that thing.

ALICE: An accident? Edward had an accident. His accident was he accidentally became close to someone else, while he was married to me. An odd sort of accident, that. Mine will be better. More colourful.

JAMIE: If you're saying all this to frighten me, then I'm frightened, okay? You have my attention. What is it you want?

ALICE: Oh, you know, this and that. We've been over it so many times, don't you think?

JAMIE: Can I see your anthology? I'd love to read it.

(ALICE *clutches the file tight, as if to stop him taking it from her.*)

ALICE: I'm not gaga yet, Jamie.

JAMIE: I didn't say you were.

ALICE: You can see my anthology later.

JAMIE: What are you going to call it?

ALICE: I'm thinking of calling it *I Have Been Here Before*. That's rather the point, you see. Others have been through these things before us. I don't know why that should be comforting, but it is. It's the first line of a poem by Dante Gabriel Rossetti. Do you know it?

JAMIE: No.

ALICE: Do you want to hear it?

JAMIE: Yes. I'd like that.

(*As she speaks the poem, her attention turns away from* JAMIE, *and she moves slowly towards the shadowed figure of* EDWARD.)

ALICE: *I have been here before,*
        But when or how I cannot tell:
        I know the grass beyond the door,
        The sweet keen smell,
The sighing sound, the lights around the shore.

        You have been mine before,—
        How long ago I may not know:
        But just when at that swallow's soar
        Your neck turned so,
Some veil did fall,—I knew it all of yore.

        Has this been thus before?
        And shall not thus time's eddying flight
        Still with our lives our love restore
        In death's despite,
And day and night yield one delight once more?

(*Lights fade on* JAMIE.)

(*Lights come up on* EDWARD. *He's gazing at* ALICE *as she moves towards him.*)

(*She comes to a stop before him, with the file in her hands, looking at him.*)

EDWARD: Yes. I realise now that you're here that I've been expecting you.

ALICE: Well. Here I am.

(*She looks round.*)

> In this truly repellent room. Edward, how can you bear to live here?

EDWARD: It does the job.

ALICE: But the wallpaper! Doesn't it make you ill?

EDWARD: I can't say I notice it.

(ALICE *moves about the room, appalled.*)

ALICE: Magazine rack. Breakfast bar. Picture window. All so very— what was your word?—sunny. Is your life sunny now, Edward?

EDWARD: Don't do this, Alice.

ALICE: Jamie tells me you're moving. To Durham.

EDWARD: Yes.

ALICE: So this may be our last meeting.

EDWARD: It may.

ALICE: My last chance to—(*letting it hang there*)—to give you this.

(*The file. But she doesn't hold it out to him.*)

EDWARD: What is it?

ALICE: My anthology. I've finished it. I thought you might like to have it.

EDWARD: Why me?

ALICE: You used to like my poems.

EDWARD: Yes. I did.

ALICE: Or was that just another of your lies?

EDWARD: No. I can even remember the odd line.

ALICE: Can you? Give me the odd line.

(EDWARD *searches his memory.*)

EDWARD: *And now in age I bud again,*
    After so many deaths I live and write;
        I once more smell the dew and rain,
    And—and—

(*That's as far as he can get.* ALICE *finishes it for him.*)

ALICE: *And relish versing: O my only light,*
            It cannot be
            That I am he
    On whom thy tempests fell all night.

EDWARD: I don't have your memory, of course. But bits have stuck.

ALICE: I had no idea.

(*She moves to one of the chairs, and sits down.*)

ALICE: I'm sorry I was rude about the house. It's your home now.
    I don't think I'll ever have a home again. Not till I die.

EDWARD: Then at least you get to choose the wallpaper.

ALICE: Was that a joke?

EDWARD: Not much of one.

ALICE: I don't think I've ever heard you make a joke before. You must be happy.

EDWARD: I think I am.

ALICE: And I've become the past, haven't I? Your life with me just—a wrong turning.

EDWARD: I did think that. For a while. But it's not true. We were together thirty years. Whoever I am now is partly you. And always will be.

ALICE: You're there now. You never used to be there. How strange it all is.

(*She holds out the file. He takes it and sits down in the other chair. He opens the file.*)

EDWARD: There's a knife here.

ALICE: Oh, yes. I forgot.

(*She holds out her hand once more, this time for the knife. He reaches it across to her. She holds it up and turns it this way and that, so that it catches the light.*)

I had an idea I might kill myself.

EDWARD: Alice—

(*She puts the knife down.*)

ALICE: But I suppose I'll go on.

(EDWARD *looks back at the anthology. He starts turning the pages. He speaks softly, not looking up at her, reading one of the poems.*)

EDWARD: *The fields are full of summer still*
    And breathe again upon the air
    From brown dry side of hedge and hill
    More sweetness than the sense can bear.

    So some old couple—

(*He stops, unable to go on.* ALICE, *of course, knows it by heart.*)

ALICE: *So some old couple, who in youth*
    With love were filled and over-full,
    And loved with strength and loved with truth,
    In heavy age are beautiful.

(*Lights go down on* ALICE *and* EDWARD.)

(*Lights come up on* JAMIE. *He goes to the shadowed figure of* ALICE.)

JAMIE: I had hoped to be able to help you, but in the end all I can do is honour you. My mother, first among women. My own true god. My warmth and my comfort, my safety, my pride. You are the one I want to please. You are the one I want to applaud me. All other women are made in your image, but not being you, are imperfect, undesirable. You are gallant, and strong, and sure. You can carry me in your arms. In your warm unfailing arms. You carry me. How can the child bear your unhappiness?

(*He turns to* EDWARD.)

My father, first among men. The man I want to be. The man I know I will become. When you kiss me, your face scratches me softly, a promise of power that will never hurt me. I believe in your justice, and your goodness. Still today I feel it to be true, untouched by all the evidence of my later life: women love, and men are good. Women love, badly, and men are good, but don't love.

(*He moves around them, speaking now to them both.*)

When we walked on the Downs, you strode ahead of me, side by side, over the bouncing land, and I ran after you. You grow older now, but you're still ahead of me, as you'll always be. For ever further down the road. My beloved explorers. As you suffer, so I shall suffer. As you endure, so I shall endure. Forgive me for worshipping you. Forgive me for needing you to be strong for ever. Forgive me for being your child.

(*Lights fade on* JAMIE, *and all is dark once more.*)

APPENDIX: POEMS QUOTED IN THE PLAY
▼ ▼ ▼

THE IMPULSE
by Robert Frost

It was too lonely for her there,
    And too wild,
And since there were but two of them,
    And no child,

And work was little in the house,
    She was free,
And followed where he furrowed field,
    Or felled tree.

She rested on a log and tossed
    The fresh chips,
With a song only to herself
    On her lips.

And once she went to break a bough
    Of black alder.
She strayed so far she scarcely heard
    When he called her—

And didn't answer—didn't speak—
    Or return.

She stood, and then she ran and hid
   In the fern.

He never found her, though he looked
   Everywhere,
And he asked at her mother's house
   Was she there.

Sudden and swift and light as that
   The ties gave,
And he learned of finalities
   Besides the grave.

TWO IN THE CAMPAGNA
by Robert Browning

I wonder do you feel to-day
   As I have felt since, hand in hand,
We sat down on the grass, to stray
   In spirit better through the land,
This morn of Rome and May?

For me, I touched a thought, I know,
   Has tantalized me many times,
(Like turns of thread the spiders throw
   Mocking across our path) for rhymes
To catch at and let go.

Help me to hold it! First it left
   The yellowing fennel, run to seed
There, branching from the brickwork's cleft,
   Some old tomb's ruin: yonder weed
Took up the floating weft,

Where one small orange cup amassed
   Five beetles,—blind and green they grope

Among the honey-meal: and last,
   Everywhere on the grassy slope
I traced it. Hold it fast!

The champaign with its endless fleece
   Of feathery grasses everywhere!
Silence and passion, joy and peace,
   An everlasting wash of air—
Rome's ghost since her decease.

Such life here, through such lengths of hours,
   Such miracles performed in play,
Such primal naked forms of flowers,
   Such letting nature have her way
While heaven looks from its towers!

How say you? Let us, O my dove,
   Let us be unashamed of soul,
As earth lies bare to heaven above!
   How is it under our control
To love or not to love?

I would that you were all to me,
   You that are just so much, no more.
Nor yours nor mine, nor slave nor free!
   Where does the fault lie? What the core
O' the wound, since wound must be?

I would I could adopt your will,
   See with your eyes, and set my heart
Beating by yours, and drink my fill
   At your soul's springs,—your part my part
In life, for good and ill.

No. I yearn upward, touch you close,
   Then stand away. I kiss your cheek,
Catch your soul's warmth,—I pluck the rose

And love it more than tongue can speak—
Then the good minute goes.

Already how am I so far
   Out of that minute? Must I go
Still like the thistle-ball, no bar,
   Onward, whenever light winds blow,
Fixed by no friendly star?

Just when I seemed about to learn!
   Where is the thread now? Off again!
The old trick! Only I discern—
   Infinite passion, and the pain
Of finite hearts that yearn.

THE COLLAR
by George Herbert

I struck the board, and cried, 'No more!
                  I will abroad.
  What? shall I ever sigh and pine?
My lines and life are free; free as the road,
  Loose as the wind, as large as store.
       Shall I be still in suit?
  Have I no harvest but a thorn
  To let me blood, and not restore
  What I have lost with cordial fruit?
                Sure there was wine
Before my sighs did dry it: there was corn
       Before my tears did drown it.
  Is the year only lost to me?
       Have I no bays to crown it?
No flowers, no garlands gay? all blasted?
          All wasted?
  Not so, my heart: but there is fruit,

And thou hast hands.
Recover all thy sigh-blown age
On double pleasures: leave thy cold dispute
Of what is fit, and not. Forsake thy cage,
Thy rope of sands,
Which petty thoughts have made, and made to thee
Good cable, to enforce and draw,
And be thy law,
While thou didst wink and would not see.
Away; take heed:
I will abroad.
Call in thy death's head there: tie up thy fears.
He that forbears
To suit and serve his need,
Deserves his load.'
But as I raved and grew more fierce and wild
At every word,
Methoughts I heard one calling, 'Child!'
And I replied, 'My Lord'.

THE CONFIRMATION
by Edwin Muir

Yes, yours, my love, is the right human face.
I in my mind had waited for this long,
Seeing the false and searching for the true,
Then found you as a traveller finds a place
Of welcome suddenly amid the wrong
Valleys and rocks and twisting roads. But you,
What shall I call you? A fountain in a waste,
A well of water in a country dry,
Or anything that's honest and good, an eye
That makes the whole world bright. Your open heart,
Simple with giving, gives the primal deed,
The first good world, the blossom, the blowing seed,

The hearth, the steadfast land, the wandering sea,
Not beautiful or rare in every part,
But like yourself, as they were meant to be.

OZYMANDIAS
by Percy Bysshe Shelley

I met a traveller from an antique land
Who said: 'Two vast and trunkless legs of stone
Stand in the desert. Near them, on the sand,
Half sunk, a shattered visage lies, whose frown,
And wrinkled lip, and sneer of cold command,
Tell that its sculptor well those passions read
Which yet survive, stamped on these lifeless things,
The hand that mocked them and the heart that fed;
And on the pedestal these words appear:
"My name is Ozymandias, king of kings:
Look on my works, ye Mighty, and despair!"
Nothing beside remains. Round the decay
Of that colossal wreck, boundless and bare
The lone and level sands stretch far away.'

MADELEINE IN CHURCH
by Charlotte Mew

How old was Mary out of whom you cast
So many devils? Was she young or perhaps for years
She had sat staring, with dry eyes, at this and that man going past
Till suddenly she saw you on the steps of Simon's house
And stood and looked at you through tears.
I think she must have known by those
The thing, for what it was that had come to her.
For some of us there is a passion, I suppose

So far from earthly cares and earthly fears
That in its stillness you can hardly stir

Or in its nearness, lift your hand,
So great that you have simply got to stand
Looking at it through tears, through tears.
Then straight from these there broke the kiss,
I think you must have known by this
The thing, for what it was, that had come to you:
She did not love you like the rest,
It was in her own way, but at the worst, the best,
She gave you something altogether new.
And through it all, from her, no word,
She scarcely saw you, scarcely heard:
Surely you knew when she so touched you with her hair,
Or by the wet cheek lying there,
And while her perfume clung to you from head to feet all through
the day
That you can change the things for which we care,
But even you, unless you kill us, not the way.

This, then, was peace for her, but passion too.
I wonder was it like a kiss that once I knew,
The only one that I would care to take
Into the grave with me, to which if there were afterwards, to wake.
Almost as happy as the caravan dead
In some dim chancel lying head to head
We slept with it, but face to face, the whole night through—
One breath, one throbbing quietness, as if the thing
behind our lips was endless life,
Lost, as I woke, to hear in the strange earthly
dawn, his 'Are you there?'
And lie still, listening to the wind outside, among the firs.

So Mary chose the dream of Him for what was left to
her of night and day,
It is the only truth: it is the dream in us
That neither life nor death nor any other thing can take away:
But if she had not touched Him in the doorway of her dream
Could she have cared so much?

She was a sinner, we are but what we are:
The spirit afterwards, but first, the touch.

DOVER BEACH
by Matthew Arnold

The sea is calm to-night.
The tide is full, the moon lies fair
Upon the straits;—on the French coast the light
Gleams and is gone; the cliffs of England stand,
Glimmering and vast, out in the tranquil bay.
Come to the window, sweet is the night-air!
Only, from the long line of spray
Where the sea meets the moon-blanched land,
Listen! you hear the grating roar
Of pebbles which the waves draw back, and fling,
At their return, up the high strand,
Begin, and cease, and then again begin,
With tremulous cadence slow, and bring
The eternal note of sadness in.

Sophocles long ago
Heard it on the Ægæan, and it brought
Into his mind the turbid ebb and flow
Of human misery; we
Find also in the sound a thought,
Hearing it by this distant northern sea.

The Sea of Faith
Was once, too, at the full, and round earth's shore
Lay like the folds of a bright girdle furled.
But now I only hear
Its melancholy, long, withdrawing roar,
Retreating, to the breath
Of the night-wind, down the vast edges drear
And naked shingles of the world.

Ah, love, let us be true
To one another! for the world, which seems
To lie before us like a land of dreams,
So various, so beautiful, so new,
Hath really neither joy, nor love, nor light,
Nor certitude, nor peace, nor help for pain;
And we are here as on a darkling plain
Swept with confused alarms of struggle and flight,
Where ignorant armies clash by night.

AUTUMN
by Rainer Maria Rilke, translated by Hope Rosenthal

A sensation of falling is not unique or new.
My failing falling hand
Has got the falling sickness even Caesar
Could not withstand.
Yet underneath I know another hand
A falling universe cannot fall through.

SUDDEN LIGHT
by Dante Gabriel Rossetti

I have been here before,
        But when or how I cannot tell:
I know the grass beyond the door,
        The sweet keen smell,
The sighing sound, the lights around the shore.

You have been mine before,—
        How long ago I may not know:
But just when at that swallow's soar
        Your neck turned so,
Some veil did fall,—I knew it all of yore.

Has this been thus before?
  And shall not thus time's eddying flight
Still with our lives our love restore
  In death's despite,
And day and night yield one delight once more?

THE FLOWER
by George Herbert

How fresh, O Lord, how sweet and clean
Are thy returns! even as the flowers in spring,
  To which, besides their own demean,
The late-past frosts tributes of pleasure bring,
      Grief melts away
      Like snow in May,
  As if there were no such cold thing.

Who would have thought my shrivelled heart
Could have recovered greenness? It was gone
  Quite underground; as flowers depart
To see their mother-root, when they have blown;
      Where they together
      All the hard weather,
  Dead to the world, keep house unknown.

These are thy wonders, Lord of power,
Killing and quickening, bringing down to hell
  And up to heaven in an hour;
Making a chiming of a passing-bell.
      We say amiss,
      This or that is.
  Thy word is all, if we could spell.

O that I once past changing were,
Fast in thy Paradise, where no flower can wither!

Many a spring I shoot up fair,
Offering at heaven, growing and groaning thither:
      Nor doth my flower
      Want a spring shower,
My sins and I joining together.

But while I grow in a straight line,
Still upwards bent, as if heaven were mine own,
    Thy anger comes and I decline:
What frost to that? what pole is not the zone,
      Where all things burn,
      When thou dost turn,
And the least frown of thine is shown?

And now in age I bud again,
After so many deaths I live and write;
    I once more smell the dew and rain,
And relish versing: O my only light,
      It cannot be
      That I am he
On whom thy tempests fell all night.

These are thy wonders, Lord of love,
To make us see we are but flowers that glide;
    Which when we once can find and prove,
Thou hast a garden for us, where to bide.
      Who would be more,
      Swelling through store,
Forfeit their Paradise by their pride.

THE FIELDS ARE FULL
OF SUMMER STILL
by Edward Shanks

The fields are full of summer still
  And breathe again upon the air

From brown dry side of hedge and hill
   More sweetness than the sense can bear.

So some old couple, who in youth
   With love were filled and over-full,
And loved with strength and loved with truth,
   In heavy age are beautiful.